Someday I'd Write This Down

A Verse-Play
by

Lowell Jaeger

Act One: The World Spinning 'Round

Act Two: Can You Hear Me?

(Approximate running time: ninety minutes.)

Plus . . . Poet's Notes: 36 Essays for Reflection and Discussion

Cover Design: Sally Johnson

Thank you: Hannah Bissell Kauffman, Teresa Mei Chuc, Lois Red Elk, Dr. Robert "Bill" Wilmouth, Precious McKenzie, Amy Jaeger, Humanities Montana, Montana Arts Council.

ISBN-13: 978-0-692-03599-3
ISBN-10: 0-692-03599-0

Library of Congress Control Number: 2018966043

Shabda is the Sanskrit word for "sound, speech." Shabda is the sound current vibrating in all creation referred to as the Audible Life Stream, Inner Sound, and Word. Shabda Press was founded in June 2011 by Teresa Mei Chuc, with the mission to bring forth the luminous words and sounds of new, emerging, and established voices.

Published by Shabda Press, Pasadena, CA 91107 www.shabdapress.com

Acknowledgments: *Someday I'd Write This Down* originally produced by the Flathead Valley Community College Theatre Department — Joe Legate, Rich Haptonstall, Joshua Kelly, Cody LaPorta, Caden Just, David Reese, Julie Legate, Nick Brester, Solomon Frenchi, Caitlin Goeman, Stuart Green, Micah Groschupf, Joshua Legate, Bryan Zipp, Alyssa Nelson, and others.

Early versions of Poet's Notes Essays appeared in *Songs of Eretz Poetry Review* (Dr. Steven Wittenberg Gordon, Editor-in-Chief).

Poems in this play were originally published in the following literary journals:
Atlanta Review, Big Muddy, Briar Cliff Review, Birmingham Arts Journal, Blue Collar Review, Callapoya Collage, Concho River Review, Dos Passos Review, Forge, Front Range Review, Handful of Dust, Hanging Loose, Louisville Review, Medusa's Kitchen, Paterson Literary Review, Prairie Schooner, Raintown Review, Saxifrage Poetry Review, Songs of Eretz Poetry Review, Suisun Valley Review, The Alembic, The Boiler Journal, The Chaffey Review, The Licking River Review, The Writing Disorder, Verse-Virtual, Verse Wisconsin, West Branch.

Created, designed, and produced in the United States.
Printed in the United States.

Do-er. Watcher. Star-Child.

Someday I'd Write This Down is an exploration of consciousness — the evolution of one man's cognitive/spiritual growth from early childhood through late adulthood. But the story is larger than the depiction of one man's experience. Many of us like to think of ourselves as unique; yet, as a species, our lives resemble each other much more than not. Each of us is asking, "Who am I?" We have this basic human dilemma in common. Each of us is struggling to understand his or her place in the world. We have this dilemma in common also.

The Narrator, an old man, is the voice of hard-earned wisdom. He's scanning the trajectory of his life. Characters coming and going on the stage are ghosts inhabiting his memories. The Boy and Young Man are younger versions of the Narrator; all three are the same body and soul. In looking back, the Narrator is at times surprised, awed, and dumbfounded by what he recalls of himself and his loved ones. His memories rise and fall — some ridiculous and surreal, some rich with depth and meaning. The bell rings and characters rearrange themselves from scene to scene (one memory into the next) with exaggerated jerky motions resembling a fast-forwarded homemade film.

What is the evolution of cognitive/spiritual consciousness? In the first scene ("Some Memories Never Leave") the Boy is both falling asleep and waking to himself on a warm summer evening with the windows wide and curtains lifting and falling in the twilight breeze. His father and a neighbor, both mill laborers, have stolen for themselves an evening of fun, clinking beers and blowing on a trombone, inventing bluesy expressions of joy and sorrow. "This becomes the music of my heart," says the Boy. He recognizes himself as an individual link in the chain of human connections. He's the "Doer" — conscious of his own flesh and blood, his feet on the ground, inextricably enmeshed in circumstances which brought him here in the first place.

Young Man arrives in Act Two at the close of the poem "Hitchhiker." Young Man has awakened into a second level of consciousness, hovering above his physical self, looking earthward. He's the "Watcher," puzzled, thrilled, bemused. He's "dizzied, a-tingle" — attuned to the small events shaping his own story as part of a larger saga of humankind. He vows, "to carry with me / the joy of it all / and someday I'd write this down."

The Narrator reconstructs the arc of his life, memory by memory. In the poem "Ghosting Home" — once both his parents have passed — he walks away from his father's open grave with an enlightened heart, cognizant of life's rich possibilities and painful limitations. In the poem "Listening," his consciousness has turned skyward to the mysteries of the cosmos. Where once he marveled in the realization of his common human form, he now sits in contemplative silence, staring into the "big black empty," filled with an amalgam of wonder, pity, compassion. He's the "Star-Child," grasping the jaw-dropping grand scheme, astonished by the strange impossible reality of our tiny existence amidst a labyrinth of lights in the night sky.

What does the Star-Child know? He knows life is short and mysterious; nothing is more certain than death, nothing more precious than our human connections. He has arrived at the conundrum of King Solomon where wisdom can bring much grief, and knowledge can bring much sorrow. He clings to this faith: The truth — confounding, always — will set us free.

Characters:
.

Boy — Early consciousness (grade school through high school) of second oldest son in a Midwestern working-class family. Slight of stature, soft-spoken, bookish, observant, sensitive. Awestruck with a powerful appreciation for life's possibilities, puzzling to make sense of the world around him. Overly immersed in family difficulties. Watchful, cautious, fearful. Also, at times, curious and brave. Wears red headband which he passes to Young Man in Act Two.

Young Man — Gentle, youngish male, athletic build (military-draft age through adult). Peacenik. Acutely aware of his own shortcomings and the foibles of friends and loved ones. Still quiet, bookish, observant. An idealist with a wounded heart, still struggling to make sense of himself, his family, his world. Appears to others as somewhat separate, detached, aloof, but he's trying to fit in. Persuaded by a growing sense of irony. Cognizant of life's inconsistencies, the chasm between how things appear and how things really are. Wears red headband.

Narrator — Old Man. Observant. No longer overly-sympathetic, he's learned acceptance toward his own limitations, the limitations of his loved ones, and the difficulties of the world in general. He's saddened and bemused. At times surprised and inspired to witness the tenacity and innate wisdom of the Boy and the Young Man. Big-picture awareness. Senses both the holiness and ridiculousness of everything and everyone. Moves during each scene with script and pen in hand, taking notes, composing, reciting, revising, interacting with his memories as characters speak. Clear voice, articulate pronunciation, self-possessed demeanor. Wears purple headband. (Note: The entire play is happening in the mind of the Narrator as he composes reminiscences on paper. His memories are so vivid they seem to him real. At times, he interacts with characters — ghosts of memories — on the stage as if they were flesh and blood. Characters on stage are teaching the Narrator to see his memories in new ways, sometimes with sadness, sometimes with humor, sometimes with inspired insight.)

Father – Working-class 1950s-1960s American head of household. WWII veteran, still shell-shocked and in search of an elusive inner serenity. Weekend musician/performer, an aspiring Elvis. Somewhat of a charmer, somewhat of a child. Union leader. Overwhelmed by family demands and financial pressures. Harmonizer. Loathes conflict, longs for emotional tranquility. Baffled by his own missteps and good intentions gone wrong. Resentful of change. Gentle, yet at times filled with false bravado. Wears flannel work shirts, work boots.

Mother – Stay-at-home mom of four boys and one girl. Hard-working, yet overwhelmed, escapist, petulant, self-pitying. Emotionally unpredictable, easily upset, a bit hard to get along with. In many ways, a very nurturing/caring parent and, in many ways, not. Envious of others, yet fiercely defensive of her kin. Riddled with fear and self-doubt. At heart, a dreamer, a young girl forever. Resentful that life has handed her a raw deal. Wears an apron constantly, or is tying, untying, and re-tying her apron strings.

Wesley – Neighborhood pal. Classmate in 6th and 7th grade. Daring, charismatic, ne'er-do-well. Interested in grown-up things inappropriate to his age . . . smoking, drinking, sex. Big-talker, schemer. Hyperactive. Parents own neighborhood bar and leave Wesley unsupervised most of the time. Wears, tennis shoes, t-shirts. Hair greased and combed Elvis-style.

Extras – Three "others," who remain nameless and faceless as possible, serve fill-in roles on stage and are scripted to speak on one occasion only. These three wear grey hooded sweatshirts (hoods up) and grey sweat pants to maximize their "extra-ness" or anonymity.

Note: *Someday I'd Write This Down* is an experiment toward finding a new way to engage an audience with poems. This is a mixed-media or multi-media approach in which the audience is aesthetically stimulated from many angles at once — words, lights, colors, sounds, actions, props, etc. Yet, it's important to maintain the focus of this production on the words and contents of the poems. All stage embellishments are meant to illuminate the poems and enhance the viewer's cognitive and emotional experience of each poem's content. There are, nonetheless, moments in the script in which the poem is put aside to highlight an interaction on the stage. This is done at times for dramatic effect and at times for comic relief.

Set:

Three platforms. Tier One (8'x 10') rises 14" from stage floor and is located stage left, near center stage. Tier Two (6'x 8') rises 14" directly behind Tier One. Tier Three (6'x 8') rises 28" from Tier Two and is located stage right, adjacent to Tier Two. One step (facing audience) connects the downstage floor with Tier One. One step (facing audience) connects Tier One to Tier Two. Three steps (right side of Tier Two) connect Tier Two to Tier Three. Steps are also located behind Tier Two (invisible to audience) and are used for character exits off stage.

White, gauzy curtains, hung behind the three tiers, serve as a screen for projected poem titles and backdrops.

Lighting: Spotlights and effects vary as needed.

Props:

The following props are placed before play begins, all visible to audience. Some props move from scene to scene as detailed in the script. Some props remain stationary.

1.) Downstage:

—Rocking chair, stage left. Chair is angled toward stage right, such that the face of someone
       sitting in the chair can be seen by the audience and also seen by characters on the stage.
—Tombstone (simple in design) located to the right of center stage, facing audience.
       Tombstone inscribed as follows: Front (viewed by audience during Act One) – "Do Not
       Ask . . ." and back (viewed by audience during Act Two) "It Tolls for Thee."
— Two brooms, upright, leaning against step from Tier One to Tier Two. Broom handles are
       embellished with ribbons or strips of colorful cloth.
— A moveable (on wheels) wooden box to be used as a dining table, rowboat, and other
       purposes as needed.

2.) Tier One:

— Trombone set upright in stand on left side downstage edge of tier.
— Two beer bottles set upright near the trombone stand.

3.) Tier Two:

— Sleeping bag unrolled to the right side of tier, near the downstage edge.
— Pillow (smallish, plump, same cloth as Mother's apron) at head of sleeping bag.
— Large window frame set upright at far left upstage side of tier. Gauzy white curtains hung on
       each side of the window frame facing downstage.

Note: Set design, props, and lighting can be altered at the director's discretion to achieve many and various impressions. As playwright, I'm attracted to a more surreal and dreamy atmosphere for this drama, since the action takes place in the Narrator's memory and memories can be tainted and slippery.

	Sounds	**Images**
Opening of Act One:	— The Beatles, "Fool on the Hill."	
"Some Memories Never Leave"	— Trombone blues line. — Clinking beer bottles.	Gauzy white curtains gently billowing.
"Buzz-Cut Saturdays"	— Buzz of hair clippers.	Country kitchen.
"Bull-Headed"	— Muffled heartbeat.	Pale blue sky with clouds.
"Working on My Words"	— Muffled gasping. — Labored breathing.	Old-fashioned country parlor.
"She Didn't Like What She Didn't Know"	— Light wind and rain.	Same country parlor.
"Bath Time!"	— Crickets and birds.	Old-fashioned bath tub/bathroom.
"Washday, Everyday"	— Winter winds blowing.	Country kitchen again.
"Seim's Bottle Gas"	— Muffled radio static.	Dusty backroad.
"Slugs (1963)"	— Construction noise.	Edge of town construction site.
"You Be Good"	— Glasses clinking. — Muffled chatter.	A dive bar.
"Holy Cow!"	— None.	None.
"Great Aunt Ida's Last Christmas"	— TV static. — Low murmuring TV show.	Large black-and-white TV screen.
"How We Survived the Cuban Missile Crisis"	— Distant air-raid siren.	Mushroom cloud unfolding.
"The Cold War at Home"	— Winter winds blowing.	Country kitchen again.
"Peace"	— Far off machine gun.	WWII combat scene. Machine-gunner.
"Broke"	— Winter winds blowing.	Country kitchen again.
"The Test"	— Geiger Counter crackling.	Mushroom cloud (static).
Closing of Act One:	— The Beatles, "Rain."	

Note: A meditation bell chimes to open each scene. Ringing echoes, then fades to silence while characters position themselves, props move, and screen and lighting change. Reading begins when chime ends.

Sounds		Images
Opening of Act Two:	— Crosby, Stills, Nash, & Young, "Find the Cost of Freedom."	
"Things Got Worse"	— Blizzard winds.	Blowing snow.
	— Trombone blues line.	
"Wesley's Playland"	— Muffled laughter.	Large colorful jukebox.
"Weasel Shit"	— Crickets and birds.	An empty cow pasture.
"Lewis and Clark the Hard Way"	— Crickets and birds.	River flowing.
"Murder"	— Distant train whistle.	Rural train trestle.
"Goodbye Wesley"	— Crickets and birds.	Forest meadow, river.
"Let's Hope This Thing Blows over Soon"		
	— Cold wind blowing.	Military cemetery.
	— Rifle salute.	
"Hitchhiker"	— Whispering breezes.	Bright sun.
		Distant high-desert mountains.
"Let's Get Stupid"	— None.	Mill smokestacks.
"Action"	— Muffled marching.	Peace march. (Static photo.)
	— Marching morphs into clock ticking.	Stuck needle on stereo.
"Kissing"	— Blowing snow.	Blowing snow.
	— Dog panting.	
"You Don't Sound So Good"	— Phone ringing.	Long distance telephone lines.
"Change Finds My Hometown"	— Cold winds again.	Country kitchen again.
"Thirty-five Years"	— Clock ticking.	Mill smokestacks.
"Sentimental Value"	— Muffled heartbeat.	Country kitchen again.
"Someone Needs to Keep Track"	— Clock ticking.	Country kitchen again.
"The Pillow"	— None.	Black night. Stars.
"Ghosting Home"	— None.	Black night. Stars.
"Listening"	— Faint ocean waves.	Oregon beach photo.
Closing of Act Two:	—The Beatles, chorus from "Hey Jude."	

Note: Various sound effects and character voices (as detailed in the script) are issued as if from a loud, invisible voice in the sky. (This can be toyed with to generate surprise, mystery, awe, humor, etc.) This also is used to include voices in the poems which are not cast as characters on the stage.

Someday I'd Write This Down

by

Lowell Jaeger

Table of Contents:

Someday I'd Write This Down

Act One: The World Spinning 'Round

Some Memories Never Leave

Mid-summer evening, hot enough
to lie in bed with windows wide
to storms billowing in the distant west.
Curtains filling with breezes,
exhaling and falling slack.

I'm half awake, listening to the neighbor
across the street. He's drinking
tonight's twelve pack, sharing one
with my father who couldn't resist
walking over to tell a joke, same joke

he told my oldest brother earlier
and the supermarket checkout clerk
before that and the butcher
before that. Everyone laughs,
but I don't get it. I've just passed

kindergarten and I don't get it; I do
know at least that. Now
they are blowing on a trombone,
the neighbor and my father taking turns
inventing slow mellow blues refrains

so sad they drip with joy. *This
becomes the language of my heart.* How
these men squeeze in a little laughter
between shifts at the mill. Making
music barefoot in their undershorts

on the curb. Clinking their empties
in the trash. The curtains filling
and falling. I haven't mastered yet
worries beyond what reaches me
through an open window half-dreaming.

The sorrowful trombone feels right.
I let it slide into me line by line,
make room for it in that place
where some memories lodge and never leave.

While so many rush past and never look back.

(Act One opens with The Beatles: "Fool on the Hill.")

Bell — lights fade.
> — characters position themselves.
> — screen: curtains billowing.

Narrator asleep in rocking chair, manuscript on his lap.
Boy enters, nudges Narrator awake. Narrator wraps his
blanket around Boy and guides him up to Tier Three
where sleeping bag and pillow await him.

Father and Extra sitting on edge of Tier One, clinking beer
bottles. Extra holds trombone.

Narrator begins reading/writing.

* Laughter

** Trombone blues line sounds here.
Boy sits up, listens.

*** Boy looks up at Narrator. Says: *This becomes the
language of my heart.* Narrator, bemused, repeats line and
continues.

**** Father and Extra clink beer bottles.

***** Boy rises, takes red headband from Narrator, ties it
around his head, reclines again. Narrator finishes poem.

Lights fade to black.

Buzz-Cut Saturdays

Oldest first, youngest last . . . Dad sat us down
on the kitchen stool, wrapped a dish towel
around our shoulders and clipped our heads
with an electric shears, a skill he'd practiced
in boot camp on buddies from his platoon.

No complaining, Dad cautioned,
And hold still, or you'll get nicked.
We inhaled and held ourselves still as stone.
The clipper's teeth pinched and bit, drew blood
enough Dad doctored us with wet rags and pep-talks.
Take your pains like a man, he'd say.
Be tough like a soldier. He told us about the good

soldier — both legs ripped with shrapnel —
who'd inched back to the trenches, limping
bravely through a fire-fight, a wounded
comrade or two in tow. *Your scrapes are nothing
to cry about,* he'd say. And this felt comforting to us,
in a secret sissy way, caused us
to grit our teeth, puff our chests, do our best

to master Dad's expectations. Good to have him
home the whole day. Good to feel his hands
bracing our craniums, taking care to keep his cuts even.

And later on he'd parade us into the street for a few rounds
of hot grounders and pop-flies, our scabs

like badges of courage beneath our baseball caps.

Bell — characters position themselves.
    — sound: buzz of hair-clippers.
    — screen: country kitchen.

Father sitting on edge of Tier Two. Boy
sitting at Father's feet, facing audience.

* Father (crying out to the audience): *Oldest
   first, youngest last!*

** Father: *No complaining!*
*** Father: *And hold still . . . or you'll get
   nicked.*

**** Father: *Take your pains like a man . . .*
***** Father: *Be tough like a soldier!*

****** Father: *Your scrapes are nothing to
   cry about.*

Buzz gets louder.

Baseball is tossed to Narrator from off stage.
Narrator lobs ball to Boy.

Buzz fades.
Lights go black.

Bell — characters position themselves.
— sound: muffled heartbeat.
— screen: pale blue sky with clouds.

Tier One — Father with broom as fishing pole, facing away from Boy on Tier Two.

Boy watching Father closely.

Bull-Headed

Jerk 'em, Dad said, when a bullhead
tugged a bobber under and swam
for deeper bottoms farther from shore.
Look at 'em fight, Dad said,
as we heaved from muddy depths
a slick black fish thrashing thin air.

* *Father* (As he struggles with pole): *Jerk 'em!*

** Father: *Look at 'em fight!*

Had to admire the frenzy: fish
flip-flopping in the grass, Dad's
hopping hot-foot pursuit, till
he'd boot-stomped the fish stupid
long enough to rip the barb from its jaw.
Or the hook snapped like a brittle stick
in the fish's clamped steely smirk.

Don't touch the bastard, Dad said.
My brothers and I stood close,
wincing when the bullhead's quick spines
cut Dad's thumb to bleed.
Had to admire the monster's huff, gills gasping
in the catch-bucket, beady eyes glazed
light-blinded and still staring back.

*** Father: *Don't touch the bastard!*

Boy crouches closer behind Father for better view.

Admired him even worse, when Dad
nailed him to a chunk of two-by-six
— a twelve-penny spike through his brain —
and still he twitched and refused
to quit. Dad slit him, grabbed the rubbery hide
with a pliers and stripped it back. Axed

Father nailing fish to cutting board.

the bull's head clean from the rest
of its connections. And still the gills
opened a little and closed. Opened
and closed. In a heap of entrails,
a heart the size of a wart, determined
it would not stop beating.

Boy, amazed, looks to Narrator, points to fish.

Heartbeat gets louder, then fades.

Lights fade to black.

4

Bell — characters position themselves.
    — sound: muffled gasping, labored
        breathing.
    — screen: old-fashioned country parlor.

Father in rocking chair, reading newspaper, smoking. Boy sits on edge of Tier One, writing in a notebook.

Narrator staring at Father, as if begging him to do something.

Working on My Words

Working on my words, is what I called
the scribble of soft lead
I pressed into the tablet's
oversized, wide-ruled lines.
What are you doing? he asked, and I answered
without lifting my head bent
low over each pencil stroke
cramped in my determined hand.

* Boy (staring abstractly): *Working on my words.*

** Father (annoyed, looks over boy's shoulder):
    What are you doing?

So many words I didn't know
what my father meant
by his sighs in the silence
of his mother's parlor, where we lasted
that night listening to her breathe
and pass, finally, into the darkness
beyond the dark where I shuddered
to hear her gasp in an adjacent room.

*** Boy (looking to Narrator): *So many words!*
Narrator repeats line and continues.

**** Gasping from adjacent room offstage, stage
right. Father and Boy both look up and listen
with dread.

I copied my older brother's first-grade reader,
page for page, letter by big block letter
of every word I hadn't learned.
I just wanted to get it all down.
See the ball? Run, jump, play.
It seemed like important work.
While my father sat beneath the lamp
with yesterday's news concealing his face,
cigarettes wasting in the ashtray,
and his coffee — half-cup by half-cup —
gone bitter beside him.

And what I want to know, now better than
six decades after she died, is how I'd been the one
drafted to struggle through that long night
of my father's gloom. I had brothers, safe
in their beds at home. And a mother I can't remember
as ever having remembered I might be shook
out of my fragile wits having watched my father's
helplessness as he watched his mother die.

I'd packed my tablets and pencils and brother's
school books — which may well have been his bribe
that I go, not he. Yet, I suspect
I'd volunteered, a good soldier, posting
guard over my father's ordeal. Why else
would a mother let her son leave?
Maybe I'd insisted. Maybe my father
wanted me inside that terrible night
like his mother wanted her son. No one
should be alone at a time like that.

So there should have been three altogether.
But one lay in the darkness of the next room,
breathing low and uneven, as the steam heat
in that old homestead hissed and banged,
and finally she'd piped her last.

                                      * A gasp from the sky. A pause. Boy looks up at father. Boy clutches notebook to his chest.

My father — his mother's kid
in his mother's house — can't be blamed
I felt so all by myself, much as she must have
and he did too, when he returned
from her room and I could tell by the quake
in his voice our vigil was through.
What are you doing? he asked.

                                      ** Father (a bit less harsh than earlier): *What are you doing?*

Working on my words, I said.
It seemed like important work.
See the ball? Run, jump, play.
So many words I hadn't puzzled out yet.

                                      *** Boy: *Working on my words.* Father looking toward adjacent room offstage, stage right, seems not to hear.

                                      **** Boy (looking to Narrator for help): *So many words!* Narrator repeats line and continues.

At his mother's bedside,
I clutched my tablets and pencils safe
against my chest. Only the moon
lit that room. Through gauze curtains
shadows of branches danced, and she lay like a stone
washed up in the cutbank, abandoned there.

I had baby brothers and was bigger than that.
But I wanted my father to hold me
and take me away somewhere.
He lifted the dead woman's hand
and stroked her hair.

                                      Lights fade to black.

Bell — characters position themselves.
      — sound: light wind and rain.
      — screen: same country parlor.

Father packing boxes on Tier Two.
Mother, Tier One, studying small box in her hand.
Boy behind window frame, watching.

She Didn't Like What She Didn't Know

Mom found it in the kitchen cupboards.
A little jewelry box felted black with gold
latch and trim. Dad's mother had passed
and we were rummaging in the ruins
of the old farmhouse, packing
what might be worth something and burning the rest.

Inside the box lay one blonde curl,
perfumed hair. *Whose is this,* Mom asked,
whose? Dad shrugged and went on sorting
tubs of scrub rags, a steady rain
of dust floating in on scattered sunbeams
through torn curtains and murky glass.
And smoke from the fire my brothers
tended outside. Mom scowled

    * Mother: *Whose is this?*
    ** Mother: *Whose?*

a lot of late, and Dad did his best
to keep out of her way. *Must be important,*
Mom said, *if someone kept it all these years.*
Dad squirmed like he'd snagged one foot
in a trap. He'd been promoted
from crew foreman to an office job.
He smelled like cologne in the mornings
instead of sawdust. *Could be anyone's hair.*
Could be no one we know. Could be mine,
he said without turning to face her.

    *** Mother: *Must be important . . .*
       . . . if someone kept it all these years.

    **** Father: *Could be anyone's hair. Could be no*
       one we know. Could be mine.

You were blonde? Mom said.
I think so, Dad answered. Both of them
hushed to hide from us whatever it was
ready to combust between them.
Something about office floozies filing invoices
too nearby. Dad lifted a wooden crate of kitchen tools
and escaped outside. Mom studied the box,
opening and closing, touching the lock of hair
as if she were testing it to come alive.

    ***** Mother: *You were blonde?*
    ****** Father: *I think so.*

Scene closes with Father lifting a box, pausing to
see Boy behind window. Father ignores Boy, exits
Tier Two upstage.

Mother left studying the box in her hand.
Dim spotlight stays on Mother.

Boy steps down from Tier Two, takes box from
Mother, positions himself downstage, stage left.
Mother, agitated, takes broom, begins sweeping.

Lights remain.

Bell — characters position themselves.
— sound: crickets and birds.
— screen: bathroom, old-fashioned
bathtub.
Mother sweeping on Tier One.
Boy, downstage, stage left.

"Bath Time!"

Bath time! Mom called into empty fields
surrounding our house. Day had fallen
so dim we'd lost sight of fly balls in the twilight,
and reluctantly my brothers and I filed home
from far corners of play
toward our once-a-week bath —
where Mom kneeled beside the tub and scrubbed us
with sudsy gusto, same as kettles and pans.

* Mother (calling into the distance): *Bath time!*

Window on stage backlit to silhouette boy and
mother scrubbing him.

One fill of hot water for four boys
meant the water faded darker grey
the longer the last of us waited. *Cleanliness,*
Mom said, *is next to godliness.* We were blessed
with a glorious lack of both,

** Mother: *Cleanliness . . .*
*** Mother: *. . . is next to Godliness.*

except for our Saturday night soap extravaganzas
and a forced march to Sunday School
next sunrise, where the sermon suffocated us
in our buttoned collars and stiff shoes.
All of us soiled with sin from first breath,
the preacher scolded.
　　　　　Dirty as worms in the Lord's eyes.

**** Voice from sky (booming): *All of us
soiled with sin from first breath . . .*
***** Voice from sky: *Dirty as worms in the
Lord's eyes.*

None of us felt much joy till we drove home
and our hearts lifted to slip back into
yesterday's ragged jeans and smelly sneakers.
Mom laughed. Said, *I'll need to scrape your filth
off the porcelain with a putty knife.* Said,
*Now get out of my hair and don't track dirt
in the house.* Hard to believe

****** Mother: *I'll need to scrape your filth
off the porcelain with a putty knife!*
******* Mother: *Now get out my hair and
don't track dirt in the house.*
******** Boy: *So hard to believe! . . .*
Narrator repeats the line and continues.

Jehovah's spite, while Mom scoured
our grass stained t-shirts, swiped pass after pass
over scuffed linoleum. Jehovah's frown
as we dog-paddled in mud and pond scum
where we bathed naked as angels,
and later let the sun wash over us
as we tore leeches off one another's backs.

Boy looking upward, puzzled.
Mother looking downward, sweeping.

Lights fade to black.

Bell — characters position themselves.
— sound: winter winds blowing.
— screen: country kitchen.

Boy watching out window, Tier Two.

Mother enters from steps behind Tier Two.
She's cold.
Boy turns and watches as Mother comes and goes.

Washday, Everyday

Mom pinned bedsheets on the clothesline.
And laundry basket loads of dishrags
and diapers. Under a subzero sky
scrubbed ice blue. Pillowcases
and bath towels. Her breath steaming
bleached huffs. Bras and slips. Husband's
torn work pants and flannel shirts.

Her feet shushing through new snow
in Dad's oversize unzipped galoshes.
Her bare fists full of pins. Socks
and socks and socks and socks. The lines
sagged and lifted and sagged. Dad's
boxers and sister's patterned smocks. Another
pillowcase. Another pillowcase. Wind

Mother huffing and puffing.
Boy and Narrator exchange sympathetic looks.

whipping her work back at her face.
Her raw knees burned beneath a half-buttoned
battered housecoat. Her squint against
the chill and glare. Kids' school sweaters.
Underwear. Two pins for each pair.
What more should it come to other than this?
My brothers and I huddled by the stove

Mother (upset, self-pitying) picks up broom and
begins sweeping with exaggerated effort.

and shivered when she carried the outside
cold in, stamping her boots clean, clapping
her hands to warm them. Thinking now . . .
bathroom rugs. Toilet cover. This girl who'd
loved a boy from down the street. Waited
for him through the war. What more
should it come to? Her nose
red and dripping. Her ears gone blue.

Lights fade, then brighten when bell chimes.

Seim's Bottle Gas

Good news and bad banged home
the side door, etched on Dad's face.
Overtime . . . equaled extra pay;
all seven mouths of our clan
piled into the Rambler,
ventured out to the highway drive-in
for Mom's favorite root beer floats.

Layoffs . . . meant suppers fell silent early,
clink of spoon and soup bowl.
Dad's elbows on the table,
his nicotine-yellowed nails plucking stubble
till his chin bled. Mom's gaze
fixed on the butter dish.

Once, laid off for a month,
Dad swore he'd given up on the mill for good
and hired on with Seim's Bottle Gas,
gunning streets in a green pickup,
delivering propane. With school done
till fall, I could ride shotgun,
carry the clipboard on my lap,
keep track of the pen.

Seemed, to me, like a good job —
spitting gravel and dust down backroads
between cornfields, fish-tailing
up the farmer's drive. But Dad
hated it. Said, *Old Man Seim, the bastard,*
pays too low and bitches I'm slow.
If the farmer's wife offered us muffins,
how could we refuse? I'd pet a lot of dogs
and cats. Milked a cow one time.

Before the day closed with Old Man Seim
counting out his cash, Dad checked in
at the Union Hall to hear
if and when the mill would call him back.
They gonna want us again, or not? he'd say.
And before that . . . we'd be flooring it into the sunset
toward town, window vents fanning our sweaty necks,
Dad twisting the radio dials for Elvis
and crooning loud when we found him,
Love me tender, love me true.

Bell — characters position themselves.
    — sound: muffled radio static.
    — screen: dusty backroad.

Boy sits on edge of Tier One.
Father comes breezing in.

* Father: . . . *Overtime!*

Mother looks up from sweeping.

** Mother: . . . *Layoffs* . . .

Narrator coaxes boy to approach Father.

*** Boy: . . . *Can I ride shotgun?* . . .
Mother stands and turns her back to the audience.

Boy sits beside Father on movable box.
Father with hands on steering wheel.

**** Father: *Old Man Seim, the bastard, pays too*
        low. . . . Then he bitches I'm slow.

***** Father: . . . *They gonna want us back*
        again, or not? . . .

Radio static noise increases.
Boy turns, looks at Father, smiles broadly.
****** Father (crooning playfully): . . . *Love me*
        tender, love me true . . .

Lights fade, then brighten when bell chimes.

Bell — characters position themselves.
    — sound: construction noises.
    — screen: neighborhood construction site.

Slugs (1963)

Suddenly one summer our homely
little home cowered amidst bigger
constructions hammered up around us,
where once we'd roamed scattered
acres of pine like we owned them.

Bunch of rich bastards, Dad said.
He'd toss fly balls to me
and my three brothers — all of us
blocking the street when the new
neighbors honked to speed on past.

Dad would hold up his hand
like a traffic cop till his boys stood safe
at the curb. He'd swagger out of the way
stiff-necked and slow, to prove to his sons
no one should push us around.

Near dark, he'd boost us through open
windows of an unfinished split-level.
We'd kick the sawdust searching
for "slugs"— nickel-sized metal knockouts
from outlet boxes. These we'd plug in the slots
of Coke dispensers at the Piggly Wiggly after hours.

Don't tell your mom, Dad said. *She won't
like it.* We'd walk home under the stars,
glancing into lit splendors of living rooms
with color TVs and canned sound-track laughter.
They ain't so much better than we are, Dad said.
And we'd zigzag the long way home, inspecting
new construction sites,

                        each of us
clutching purloined booty — bottles of pop
trailing tell-tale sweat on the hot pave.

Father and Boy, downstage, throwing a baseball
back and forth. They pause and listen when
Narrator begins.

* Father: *. . . Bunch of rich bastards . . .*

Father holds up hand as if to direct traffic. He's
defiant.

** Father: *Don't tell your mom . . . She won't like it.*

*** Father: *They ain't so much better than we are.*

Hammering construction noises increase.
Father and Boy exit stage left, Boy following
behind Father. Boy looks at audience with a defiant
look on his face.

Lights fade to black.

You Be Good

You be good to other people, and they'll
be good back — my Dad's
creed, a true believer
in the goodness of good works.

And the goodness of work.
What you need, he'd say
is a job. And he could find you one
because he was a union man

with connections, buddies
who'd ask their boss to make room
for another man. A good man
with a wife and station wagon load of babies.

Grateful men who'd sit with him
at the bar between shifts
and buy him a round of thanks.
And another round of thanks after that.

And another.
And one, *"Jusssh for the hell of it."*
No, Dad said. *You take your money*
and go home. But the other guy
drank and drank his gratefulness tonight

and didn't want coffee, though he'd sip it
if Dad insisted. And he'd let Dad walk him
around the block. Till his head cleared
and Dad put him behind the wheel.

And waited at the curb to see him off.
You go straight home, he'd say.
Don't stop nowhere.
He'd slap the guy a little slap on one cheek.
Another slap on the other cheek.

You be good, he'd say.
Don't stop nowhere.
You got work in the morning.
Go straight home.

Bell — characters position themselves.
    — sound: glasses clinking, muffled chatter.
    — screen: a dive bar.

Father sitting on edge of Tier Two, beer in hand.
Extra standing nearby, bottle in hand. Boy watches
from outside window.

* Father (as if to audience): *You be good to other*
    people, and they'll be good back.

** Father (as if to audience): *What you need . . .*
    is a job.

Extra, drunk, teetering, facing Father.

*** Extra (drunken, slurred): *Jusssh for the hell of it.*
**** Father: *No . . . You take your money . . . and go*
    home.

Father stands, slaps drunk to sober him.

***** Father: *You go straight home . . . . Don't stop*
    nowhere.

Drunk stumbles off.

****** Father (to audience again): *You be good . . . .*
    Don't stop nowhere. You got work in the
    morning. Go straight home.

Father shakes his head sorrowfully, sits back down on
Tier Two and remains.
Lights fade, then brighten when bell chimes.

Father still sitting on edge of Tier Two,
bottle in his hand.

Boy, looking out the window, turns to
audience.

"Holy Cow!"

Mother standing, Tier One, facing audience.

Holy cow! we'd say, waking to a foot of fresh snow
covering roads and walks. Standing in our PJs barefoot
at the window, staring at drifts lolling from the eaves
like whipped cream. *Holy cow!* we'd say, pointing
at icicles bending pine branches to breaking.

* Boy: *Holy cow!*

** Boy: *Holy cow!*

Holy balls! Dad said, nodding past his beer mug
at the trophy muskie mounted behind the bar,
the open jaw spiked with rows of glinting sabers.
That sum-bitch could swallow your arm.

*** Father: *Holy balls!*

**** Father: *That sum-bitch could swallow
          your arm!*
***** Father: *Jesus balls, Man!*

Jesus balls! he'd exclaim under his breath
on days his wife and whining kids plagued him
past exasperation. *Holy flappin' balls, Man!*
meant we'd best quit yapping and keep out of his way.

****** Father: *Holy flappin' balls, Man!*

Jeez, Mom said, her bottom lip curled,
her two dollar door prize ticket winning a measly
set of plastic spoons. *Jeez, what a gyp.*
Or, *Gol darn it.*

******* Mother: *Jeez!*

******** Mother: *Jeez, what a gyp!*
******** Mother: *Gol Darn it!*

She'd plop herself down on the couch,
cross her arms and declare herself on strike.
I'm not your slave, she'd protest.
Gol darn it anyways!

********* Mother: *I'm not your slave . . .
          Gol darn it anyways!*

Mother walks off, stage left, pouting.
Father and Boy exchange a look, then shrug
sheepishly.

Lights dim. Father and Boy remain.

Great Aunt Ida's Last Christmas

Great Aunt Ida still lit candles on her Christmas tree
instead of stringing lights. Dad said, *We'd better
help her take the damn thing down before
the old homestead burns to the ground.*

Good Friday after church, we drove over
and found Great Aunt Ida in a chair pulled close
to the soaps flickering on her new TV.
He done it, she said. *I seen him. I seen him do it!*

She pointed at the black-and-white screen,
her house coat buttoned askew,
her thick ankles crushing her fuzzy slippers sideways.
That's him, she said. *He's the one.*

We raked buckets of dried needles, scraped lumps
of candle wax off the floor. Dad unscrewed the trunk
from its stand and heaved what was left
out the back door, trailing more needles and wax

and all us kids sweeping up behind him.
It's just a show, Dad shouted from across the room.
It's pretend. Aunt Ida pulled her specs
lower on her nose and fumed.

I know what I seen with my own eyes,
she said. Dad lined us up to hug the old lady
before we could go, though she never hugged back.
The room felt empty where the tree had stood.

Dad bought a round of ice cream cones
at the drive-in on our way home, and we savored
in silence, letting the cold melt on our tongues. Dad stared
ahead. *She don't know no better,* he shuddered
and mumbled more, though we didn't dare ask what.

Bell — characters position themselves.
   — screen: large black and white
      TV screen.
   — sound: low murmuring TV show
      and static.
Spotlight on rocking chair.

Father and Boy busy, sweeping.

* Father: *We'd better help her take the damn
      thing down before the old homestead
      burns to the ground.*

** Voice from sky: *He done it! . . . I seen
      him. I seen him do it!*
Father and Boy turn and look toward rocker
when Aunt Ida speaks from the sky.

*** Voice from sky: *That's him . . . he's
      the one.*

**** Father (shouting): *It's just a show!*
***** Father (shouting): *It's pretend.*

****** Voice from sky: *I know what I
      seen with my own eyes!*

Father and Boy look to audience, perplexed.

******* Father: *She don't know no better.*

Scene closes with Father shaking his head in
disbelief and frustration. He keeps shaking
his head right into the next scene. Boy
looking to audience as if for help.

Lights dim, then brighten when bell chimes.

How We Survived the Cuban Missile Crisis

Them damn Rooskies, is what Dad called the Russians,
and he spit when he said it, sick of war.
The Rooskies launched a sputnik, sailing
the stratosphere, aiming to do God-knows-what,
long before we'd figured how. And . . .
Them damn Reds, installed atomic warheads in Cuba,
Armageddon in our own backyard.

When Kennedy sent our big guns out
to stop the Cuban Commie supply line, we hid
under the basement stairs, where Mom
had shelved rows of canned beans and corn
and pickled cukes.

Little sister curled in blankets
and slept. Left us brothers hushed
and wide-eyed to worry,
huddled with nightmares of our own,
waiting for fire to come crashing.

This cold concrete floor hurts my backache,
Mom complained, and blew her nose and sniffled.
Dad hugged his radio to his ear, twisting
the antenna forward and back.

Dad listened and shushed us
for news he couldn't hear. And somewhere . . .
told Mom, *Quit your bellyaching.*
Which was enough to send her

storming upstairs. Dad sat with us
and smoldered toward an atomic blast of his own.
Oh, to hell with it,
Dad said. He scooped up little sister.
We all marched gratefully
to our regular beds, and

the Russian ships turned back toward home.

Bell — characters position themselves.
    — sound: air-raid siren in distance.
    — screen: mushroom cloud
       unfolding.

Father, Tier One, still shaking his head, a
transistor radio pressed to his ear.

Mother and Boy, downstage, sitting
uncomfortably, sharing the sleeping bag
around their shoulders.

* Father: *Them damn Rooskies!*

** Father: *Them damn Reds!*

Sirens quiet. Mushroom on screen continues
to boil.

*** Mother: *This cold concrete floor hurts my
     backache.*

**** Father: *Quit your bellyaching.*

Mother storms off, pouting. Boy looks to
Father. Father looks away.

***** Father: *Oh, to hell with it!*
Father storms off.

Boy alone, frozen.
A baby cries.

Lights fade to black.

Bell — characters position themselves.
— sound: same as last scene.
— screen: same as last scene.

Mother and Father sitting on edge of Tier One, Boy sitting between them. All using the movable box as a table.

The Cold War at Home

Ask that man to pass the potatoes,
Mom said, elbowing me to get it done.
Dad, I'd say, *please pass the potatoes.*
My parents had stepped back from the brink
of a melt-down, closed their embassies
and retreated to their own sovereign soils.

I shared a border with both quarreling
nations, and the wall between them
ran right through me. *Pass the salt,*
Dad said. Mom stiffened and pretended
not to hear. So I passed the salt.
I passed the gravy. I sent my couriers

on their bicycles, pedaling as fast as they could.
I dug a bomb shelter in my head . . .
and hunkered there, my transistor radio
pressed to my ear. So much static, so little
reliable news. Nikita and Ike slammed
doors. There was a button somewhere.

One wrong move and the planet could blow.

* Mother (petulantly): *Ask that man to pass the potatoes.*
** Boy: *. . . Dad . . . please pass the potatoes.*

*** Father (Coldly): *. . . . Pass the salt.*

***** Boy (addressing audience): *I dug a bomb shelter in my head . . .*

Screen changes to airplanes dropping bombs.

Sounds of bombs exploding.

Lights fade to black.

16

Peace

Some peace, please, Dad said. And he said it
in the tone of a man who'd earned it: *Can't we all
just mind our own damn selves and enjoy the day?*

He said it while steering the car to the lake country
up north, when we bickered in the backseat,
one brother's elbow jammed
in another brother's ribs. Brothers pulling hair till
one or the other raged in tears. Till little sister
whimpered and sobbed and couldn't stop.

He said it baiting hooks — mine, my brothers',
our sister's. *Just give me some peace, please,*
he said while untangling our lines,
working snagged barbs loose from sunken logs.

And he said it to Mom in the lawn chair behind us
on the shore when she complained about
horseflies and mosquitoes. When she slammed
her romance novel shut and stormed uphill
to sulk in the car. Where it was too hot, so
she opened the windows to horseflies and mosquitoes
who drove her back downhill to her lawn chair
where she sat red-faced and breathing fire.

He said it to his buddies at the union family picnic,
Hey, Soldiers . . . let's just all get along.
Buddies who'd drowned themselves in beer
and surfaced again swinging. Buddies who'd marched
in Patton's army; buddies who'd lugged ammo
for the big gun Dad carried and blasted
— *the whole nine yards, whole nine yards* —

.

. . . and laid to everlasting waste . . .
all of who-knows-what.

Bell — characters position themselves.
> — sound: machine-gun fire far off,
> goes silent when Father speaks first
> line.
> — screen: WWII combat scene,
> machine-gunner.

Tier One: Father using broom as fishing pole.
Mother sitting on edge of Tier Three, swatting
flies.
Boy, downstage, looking upward toward Father
and Mother.

* Father: *Some peace, please . . .*
** Father: *Can't we all just mind our own damn
selves and enjoy the day?*

Father resumes fishing.

*** Father: . . . *Just give me some peace . . .
please! . . .*

Mother resumes swatting flies.

**** Mother (agitated): . . . *Aarrgghh! . . . .*
Mother storms off, exits upstage via steps
behind Tier Two.

Muffled machine-gun fire resumes.

***** Father: *Hey, Soldiers . . . let's just all get
along!*

Machine-gun fire gets louder.

****** Father (using broom as gun): . . .
*Another whole nine yards, whole nine
yards!*
Father huffing and puffing.

Narrator looks alarmed. Boy covers his eyes.
Narrator continues.
Lights fade to black.

Bell — characters position themselves.
— sound: winter winds blowing.
— screen: country kitchen again.

Father sitting on edge of Tier Two, head in his hands.
Mother standing at window, looking out.
Boy standing downstage, looking up at parents.

Broke

That ragged winter of lost jobs at the mill,
I heard the word *welfare*   * Voice from sky (echoes): *Welfare!*
which was everywhere my father
had *gotta go,* he'd say,   * Father: . . . *Gotta go* . . .
jamming his work boots   Father still pulling his snow boots on. Exits.
into black galoshes that flapped against his ankles
because the zippers didn't work anymore than he did.

He'd nod without lifting his eyes
to my mother's whispered . . . *bye.*   *** Mother (pouting): . . . *Bye* . . . .
She'd stand at the window
with the door latched after him,
wanting him and maybe not wanting him
to turn and return
her hand's halfhearted so-long.

                              Father returns, pulls off snowboots. Sits again on
I watched his shoulders hunch   edge of Tier Two.
as he trudged out our drive,
leaning into driven snow, fists knotted
in his jacket pockets, his bristled jaw clamped.
And when he returned I heard his coat sleeves' thaw
splash on the kitchen linoleum
— each drip ticking in that charged silence —
till he tore open the blue envelope.

That's all, he'd say.   **** Father: . . . *That's all* . . .
Mother would bite her lip and look away
as he'd wad the check,
then knuckle it smooth
on the table. *Even with five kids,*   ***** Father: . . . *Even with five kids* . . .
he'd draw up his chest,
that's all they give me.   ****** Father: . . . *that's all they give me.*

Once I sat with my father on the wooden chairs
in a waiting room downtown. *I'm broke,*   ******* Father: . . . *I'm broke.*
Father told the man in the tie.
And that was true.
I'd have to get big, I guessed,
just to get through this
as day by day my father tramped
into the grey beyond our walk.   Winter winds grow louder.
And flurries blurred him.   Boy snaps his head toward audience.
Made him small.

                              Lights fade to black.

The Test

Dad confided in Mom he'd heard it
from a guy at work who'd heard it
from another guy whose younger brother
worked a maintenance job at the plant
where they built the bomb.

Reports of super-secret testing, us
against the Commies, killing the atmosphere
with radioactive dust. The air
we breathed could burn us up
from inside and turn us into lepers

with bloody sores and wrinkled skin
hanging like rags. *What if that's just talk,*
Mom said. *Maybe,* said Dad, *but what about
all those babies born wrong
with no feet or no fingers or no arms?*

Mom couldn't push that thought back.
She'd incubated four boys and wanted grandkids
someday. *I don't see how that works,*
she said. *Why is atomic fallout
making babies born wrong?* Dad shrugged.

Nobody knows, he said. And would have left it,
except Mom called us boys
into the room and looked us up and down
for worries we hadn't even dreamt of yet.
We should get 'em tested, she said.

Well, Dad said, *I think they're safe
if they got balls in the right place.*
Which is how four pre-teen boys lined up
and dropped their drawers for Dad's inspection.
What the hell, we asked. *What's going on?*

Dad bent his face close to what we'd hoped
to keep undercover. And squinched his brow.
I don't see nothin', Dad said. Mom looked
from a safe distance. She asked,
You boys feel all right?
Then threw up her arms before our reply.

How will we know, she said.
Lord, how we gonna know?

Bell . . . characters position themselves.
      — sound: Geiger Counter crackling.
      — screen: mushroom cloud (static).

Boy and three Extras lined up on downstage
edge of Tier One.

Father pacing back and forth in front of boys.
Mother standing on Tier Two, wringing her
hands in her apron.

* Mother: *. . . What if that's just talk? . . . .*
** Father: *Maybe . . . but what 'bout all those
      babies born wrong with no feet or no
      fingers or no arms? . . .*

*** Mother: *I don't see how that works . . .*
**** Mother: *. . . Why is atomic fallout making
      babies born wrong?*

***** Father: *. . . Nobody knows . . .*

****** Mother: *We should get 'em tested!*

******* Father: *Well . . . I think they're safe if
      they got balls in the right place.*

(Boy and Extras drop their pants.)
******** Boy: *What the hell . . . . What's going
      on?*

********* Father: *I don't see nothin'. . .*

********** Mother: *You boys feel all right?*

*********** Mother: *How will we know? . . .
      Lord, how we gonna know?*

Lights go black.

(Act One closes with The Beatles: "Rain.")

Someday I'd Write This Down

Act Two: Can You Hear Me?

Bell — characters position themselves.
— sound: blizzard winds.
— screen: blowing snow.

Things Got Worse

Father sitting on edge of Tier One. He's despondent, trombone in hand.
Boy on Tier Two standing to the side of Father. Boy is looking straight into the audience.
Mother standing at window, looking out, her back to everyone.

After the mill shut for good
a week before Thanksgiving, Dad
was up early with no place to go.
He'd sit with his coffee and stare
straight ahead like a blind man.
We'd come home from school and find him
still there. Then it snowed and snowed —

the roads drifted closed, trees snapped
curbside and lay broken like wounded soldiers.

* Trombone blues line. Boy snaps his head toward Father when he hears it.

Dad shouldered his shovel door-to-door
asking for work clearing drives and walks.
A nearly-grown neighbor boy did the same.
We'd report to Dad whenever we spotted the boy
slinging snow near streets Dad claimed
as his own. *He don't need it bad as I do,*

** Father: *He don't need it bad as I do . . .*

Dad said. He'd pull on his boots and storm off
muttering, *I'm gonna go see what's what
and set that boy right.*

*** Father: *I'm gonna go see what's what and set that boy right.*

A week before Christmas, Dad took a job
delivering feed and milking supplies,
and he let us ride along
to see the Christmas trim on big houses
across town. Or we'd slip and slide
county backroads delivering to farms.
A big man in coveralls loaned us an ax
and we cut a Christmas tree from his woodlot.

Boy shakes his head disapprovingly. Looks at Narrator, who also shakes his head.

Not much of a tree, I said,
and by the broken lines
on Dad's brow, I was sorry I'd said it.

**** Boy: *. . . Not much of a tree . . .*

***** Boy and Narrator exchange painful looks.

Dad lashed the sad little evergreen
to the grille of the truck, and pieces flew off
as we sped along, our snow boots caked
with manure, our noses pinched
against outhouse smells in the heat of the cab.

Trombone line again from Father. Boy snaps his head back in that direction.

At least we got food on the table, Dad said
whenever Mom looked like she felt sorry.
Or he'd say,
*There's hungry people in this world
who get on with a lot less.* Which meant
we should eat what Mom dished and not complain.

****** Father: *At least we got food on the table.*

******* Father: *There's hungry people in this world . . . who get on with a lot less.*

Lights fade to black.

Wesley's Playland

Wesley lived down the block in a different world
where his folks were hardly home because
they owned the Tic-Toc Beer Garden nearby. Wesley
invited us over to share the spoils — abandoned bottles
of gin on his mom's nightstand.

Wesley gulped shots without choking.
And smoked cigarettes like he enjoyed them,
while his pals rummaged with no worries we'd be caught
eyeballing his dad's *Playboy* foldouts
or stealing pepper sticks
from the fridge. Or blasting the basement jukebox.

Rock 'n roll, Wesley told us, *makes women crazy.*
He said it with his narrowed eyes beaming,
like he'd seen it firsthand, while the jukebox lights flashed
and boomed another new tune.
We pictured mobs of beehive blondes
swooning over Bobbie Darrin's croon.

And deeply regretted having good parents
who'd whip up a pious fuss over Wesley's playland,
where seventh-graders danced and sipped gin.
Where the only law was don't electrocute yourself
on the wet floor near the power outlets when it stormed.
Nobody touch nothin', Wesley would say,
when the jukebox threw sparks of jagged blue lightning.
This thing will kill you if you get too nearby.

Bell — characters position themselves.
　　　　— sound: muffled laughter.
　　　　— screen: large, colorful jukebox.

Wesley standing downstage, facing audience,
smoking.

Boy and Extras milling and tussling on Tier
One and Two.

Wesley continues smoking.

* Wesley: *Rock 'n Roll . . . makes women
　　crazy!*

Muffled laughter plays again until end of
scene.

Lightning flashes.

** Wesley: *. . . Nobody touch nothin' . . .*

*** Wesley: *This thing will kill you if you get
　　too nearby.*

More lightning.

Lights fade to black.

Bell — characters position themselves.
  — sound: crickets and birds.
  — screen: an empty cow pasture.

Tier One: Boy and Wesley bent over, searching.

Weasel Shit

Had he not risen up, a giant
— the old farmer in greasy coveralls —
when he parked his pickup, strode
across his pasture straight for us
and asked, *What you boys want out here;*

  * Voice from sky (booming): *What you boys want*
    out here?
  Boy and Wesley snap to attention.

had we not moments earlier crawled
under his barbed wire
and shoo-shooed his cows away;
had we not been toting fishpoles
and buckets of nothing and answered,
Huntin' frogs for bait;
and had we not been set to bolt
into the woods like rabbits when . . .

  ** Wesley: . . . *Huntin' frogs for bait.*

he wiped his brow with a rag, spit,
mumbled, *Well, gotta look in the weasel shit;*
drove off, left us guessing
as to what weasel excrement looked like
let alone where to find it and why
frogs would likely be located nearby . . .

  *** Voice from sky (booming): *Well . . . gotta look*
    in the weasel shit.

then Wesley and I might not have wasted
a sunburned afternoon poking sticks
at feces, re-inventing the science of scatology
— cow pies, dog turds, deer droppings —
but . . . *No weasel shit! No frogs! No where!*
Wesley said. And suddenly in a flash of inspiration
it struck us both, in being caught
trespassing we'd heard "weasel shit"
when, in less demanding circumstances
our ears might not have been thrumming
and we'd have decoded it right —
"Look in the weeds and shit."

  **** Wesley: . . . *No weasel shit! No frogs! Nothin'*
    no where!

  ***** Voice from sky: . . . WEASEL SHIT . . .

  ****** Voice from sky: *Look in the WEEDS AND*
    SHIT . . .
  Boy and Wesley freeze with confounded looks.

And we'd have searched down in the cattails
near the pond, found our bait,
hooked a pike or two.

  Cricket and bird sounds increase.

But now it was late toward supper
and a long, silent walk home.

  Lights fade, then brighten when bell chimes.

Lewis and Clark the Hard Way

Wesley and I read a book about Lewis and Clark
and presented in front of the class,
our eighth-grade graduation project.
Really, I read the book and told Wesley
about it, and we both told the class.
Which worked out fine because Miss Jacobson
said, *Good job, boys. You boys are really excited
about Lewis and Clark, aren't you? Maybe
you'll be explorers and make your own
discoveries someday.* Which caused us
to puff our chests and hope the girls took notice.

Also caused us to pedal up to the Lutheran Camp
with plans to steal a canoe and float the currents
back into town, though we discovered all the boats
chained up in the boathouse and had to settle
for an old rowboat abandoned in the weeds.
And we discovered our town was upstream
instead of down, and it was hard, hard work
to paddle with garden shovels because we had no oars.
Clark and Lewis, I said, *also paddled upstream.*

That's stupid, Wesley said. *Would have been easier
the other way.* We hadn't been on the water an hour,

and I was inclined to agree, as we'd discovered
twists and turns, and our destination kept creeping
farther off than we'd imagined. *Same
with Lewis and Clark,* I said. *They figured
the Pacific would be closer than it turned out.*
Wesley by this time was sunburnt and thirsty,
and we'd already gulped our Coca-Colas.
Should have looked at a map, Wesley said,
and I wasn't sure if he meant us or Lewis and Clark
though either way I could glimpse some wisdom

in that. When I joked about Injuns shooting flaming arrows
at us from shore, I discovered a dark mood
had a stranglehold on Wesley. Lots of cottonwoods, cornfields
and prairies beyond. No villages of Mandan. No antelope.
We discovered hordes of mosquitoes and horseflies.
We discovered why people employed cars these days
instead of boats. As best we could, we steered
the bow forward. Discovered arms and legs can ache
                                      like stone.

We paddled on in silence a long, long time.

Bell — characters position themselves.
       — sound: crickets and birds again.
       — screen: river flowing.

Wesley and Boy mount the movable box
as if it were a boat. Wesley in front of Boy.
Both are paddling with brooms.

* Voice from sky (female teacher): *Good
     job, boys. You boys are really excited
     about Lewis and Clark, aren't you?
     Maybe you'll be explorers and make
     your own discoveries someday.*
Wesley and Boy beaming.

Wesley and Boy stop beaming.

** Boy: *Clark and Lewis also paddled up
    stream.*
*** Wesley: *That's stupid . . . would have
    been easier the other way.*

**** Boy: *. . . Same with Lewis and Clark.
    They figured the Pacific would be
    closer than it turned out.*

***** Wesley (Peevishly): *. . . Should have
    looked at a map . . .*

Wesley and Boy continue paddling through
end of scene.

Lights fade, then brighten when bell chimes.

Bell — characters position themselves.
        — sound: distant train whistle.
        — screen: rural train trestle.

Wesley downstage. He's crouched, looking for something.
Boy standing on Tier One, nervously watching Wesley.

Murder

If he loved her, why would he kill her? I said.
Wesley stared long at me with a sorry look
like he knew something
I wasn't ready to understand. We'd found a way
along the tracks across the trestle
out to the island where they'd discovered
the young waitress, murdered. Big splash

* Boy: *If he loved her, why would he kill her?*

Wesley looks up at Boy disapprovingly. Then continues to examine the ground.

in our hometown where nothing like that happened
far back as anyone could recall. She'd crossed
the river alone after her shift one night
and never came home. Wesley and I assigned ourselves
to survey the crime scene on our own,
but happened upon a spooky loneliness,
speechless in the middle of nowhere special,
just the two of us kicking cinders

from the railroad bed into the waters below.
I'd still bet her boyfriend done it, Wesley mumbled.
They'd arrested the boyfriend but couldn't hold him,
and he'd moved back east from where he'd come.
Wesley had girlfriends, several of them already,
and I'd had none. He'd been cheated on and dumped
and dumped more. *A girl gets inside you,*
Wesley said, *to places you couldn't guess.*

** Wesley: *I'd still bet her boyfriend done it.*

*** Wesley: *. . . A girl . . . gets inside you . . .*
to places you couldn't guess . . .

Train whistle in distance.

The girl's neck was broken. She'd been stabbed,
her skull bashed with rocks. A cold wind twisted
the alders along the river bank.
Like throwing yourself under a train, Wesley said,
and he dropped face down across the rails.
He said, *Just let me lay here and die.*

**** Wesley: *Like throwing yourself under a train . . .*
***** Wesley: *Just let me lay here and die.*

I lied and pretended I'd heard a whistle coming this way.
Wesley said again, *He done it, I bet.*
And he wouldn't get back up
when I begged let's hike back across the trestles
toward town.

****** Wesley: *. . . He done it, I bet . . . .*

Train rumbling.

Lights fade to black.

Bell — characters position themselves.
      — sound: crickets and birds.
      — screen: forest, meadow, river.

Boy sitting cross-legged on Tier Two.

Goodbye, Wesley

Narrator standing at a distance. Sympathetic.

Wesley's dad sold the Tic-Toc Beer Garden
— little grey dive bar near Crockett's Trailer Court —
and Wesley moved to sunny California,
early summer of eighth-grade graduation.
We made a ceremony of it, Wesley and I,
at a campfire where the old logging road dead-ended
along river banks we'd tramped and mapped by heart.

Took a Bowie knife and slit the backsides
of our right hands enough to bleed and called ourselves
blood brothers forever. A little pain

* Boy (shows his hand): . . . *Blood brothers . . .*
      forever . . . .
** Wesley's voice from sky: . . . *Blood brothers.*

to cover over pain. *Blood brothers*
— a fit excuse to share
a stolen bottle of Boone's Farm, to kick
at flaming driftwood, watch the embers flare
and extinguish as they rose toward cold stars.

What's wrong? Mom kept asking, *What's wrong?*
I wandered in the trees most of that summer
alone, or pedaled country lanes farther and farther
outside of town, mulling over
running away to Los Angeles and knowing I'd never go.
I hammered a crude platform cradled in the forked arms
of a white pine leaning over the river. And sat
silent as muskrats paddled in the water's lasting flow.

*** Mother's voice from sky: . . . *What's*
      wrong? . . . What's wrong? . . .

Bird and cricket sounds cease. Wesley enters
stage right, downstage.

A year later, Wesley's family moved back.
I loved it there, Wesley said, *better than this place.*
His arms were freckled red and brown. He'd been trained
to mount and balance tires, and he took a grown-up job
at the new Tire Mart along the new state highway.
He was changed. Or I was changed. Or something.

**** Wesley (addressing no one): . . . *I loved it*
      there . . . better than this place.

Hey, I'd say if I saw him.
I'd wave when we passed.
He'd nod

***** Boy (holds up his hand): . . . *Hey* . . .

Wesley nods, keeps walking, exits stage left.
Boy watches him go.

and keep walking.

Lights fade to black.

Bell — characters position themselves.
      — sound: cold wind blowing.
      — screen: military cemetery.

Mother, Father, Boy, and Narrator, all standing downstage, stage left of tombstone. Two Extras standing some distance behind. Extras hold brooms like guns at attention.

Let's Hope This Thing Blows Over Soon

The Chinese, is all my father said
when my mother asked, *Who are we fighting?*
with a nuclear sunshine on the snow
so immaculate it hurt my eyes.
Three cars ahead of us and I couldn't count
how many behind, all burning
headlights and flying colors on each antenna —
yellow and black of the first funeral I ever knew.
Why? Mother kept asking, *Why?*

A dead relative. In our congressional district
where cows already outnumbered us all,
he was the first young man home in a box
from some battlefield whose name we couldn't recall.
Second cousin who took my hand years ago
as we toured his Holsteins, their stanchions locked
in a whitewashed barn larger
than my own backyard. *Watch your step,*
Watch your step, I remember him laughing,
then he shouldered me like a sack of potatoes
through the air of night, back into the living
room where our parents halted their gab, then guffawed
at the thick splash of manure under my shoes.

He died watching his step through a mine field,
though his coffin-face had forgotten,
eyebrows penciled in place, rouge
dusted on his cheeks and on his only
almost-human-looking hand. One empty black sleeve
on his dress uniform pressed and folded
neatly across his chest. I wasn't so brave
as to touch him, like most of my aunts who also
talked *how handsome* he had grown
and how just like the last war, other heroes
came home dead too. I wondered
where was that arm? Was it under water somewhere?
Might some barefoot kid harvesting rice
kick it loose and find it reaching after him nearby?

* Father: . . . *The Chinese* . . .
** Mother: . . . *Who are we fighting?* . . .

*** Mother: . . . *Why?* . . . *Why?*

**** Voice from sky (young man laughing, joyful): *Watch you step . . . watch your step . . . .*

***** Voice from sky (older woman): . . . *How handsome! . . .*

In the cemetery the sun exploded on new snow.
I followed in my father's footsteps, blinded,
careful not to stumble over bodies lying all around.
Then a short sermon to save us all
from frostbite. I let my father put the dead weight
of his arm on my shoulders. *Let's hope
this thing blows over soon,* he said,

and I knew what he was talking about,
with me in the ninth grade and a brother
old enough to drive. But I was curious
how below zero the bugler's mouthpiece
must have scorched his lips,
how the coffin slipped from its scaffold
into its concrete case with a sack-of-potatoes
thud, and when the ten-gun salute blasted the elms above,
how their icicles stabbed to the earth, shattering
the delicate safety of our lives.

****** Father: *Let's hope this thing blows
        over soon . . . .*

Extras salute and aim and shoot their brooms
skyward, ceremoniously.

Sounds of rifle salute.

Lights fade to black.

Bell — characters position themselves.
— sound: quiet, whispering breezes.
— screen: bright sun, high-desert,
mountains in distance.

Boy in sleeping bag waking on Tier Two.

Hitchhiker

No snapshot of this exists except
for the shutter of memory's random
flash impressions. So much else
went by unrecorded, almost as if
it never happened. Or — if it did —
my eyes were closed and the light shut out.

But that dawn woke with my bones
half frozen — frost on the prickly pear,
the sky pooled ice-blue,
and snowcapped distant peaks ablaze
in the early sun's glare. Three days
from home, and no one had warned me

Boy sits up, looks around, shivering.

how high-country desert nights turned
arctic, how each star looked down
with a barren stare. How I'd shiver
fitfully with hard-scrabble exhaustion
where I'd been dropped at a back-country
exit to rolling expanses of open range. How I'd rise

through misery and dance like a madman
to flush my chilled limbs with fresh
blood. How I'd laugh and fling my useless
summer-camp sleeping bag to its final
demise in a forgotten ravine. Then
shoulder my rucksack and step toward
the highway,

Boy stands, laughs, throws sleeping bag off stage.

Boy turns to Narrator.

inhaling the moment,
dizzied, a-tingle, awed by the earth at my feet,
thrilled to be my body walking, waking
amidst pungent sage, letting the sun's new rays
seep in; absolutely certain I'd carry with me
the joy of this . . .

* Boy: *Someday . . . I'll write it down!* . . .
Narrator surprised, bemused, impressed.

. . . certain I'd carry with me
the joy of it all . . .

Young Man enters, stage left. Climbs Tier One,
stands next to Boy on Tier Two. Boy hands over red
headband, reluctantly. Young Man dons headband as
Boy exits upstage. Young Man faces audience.

and someday I'd write this down.

Lights fade to black.

Bell — characters position themselves.
— sound: none.
— screen: mill smokestacks.

Young Man sitting on the edge of Tier One. He's at the steering wheel.

Let's Get Stupid

Let's get stupid, my brother
laughed with his pals, as they piled into
Dad's station wagon after school.
And passed a joint between them,
each in turn coughing, while the others
mocked and jabbed: *Pussy. You pussy!*

I kept the windows rolled down
and worried about cops. Worried
about getting in a wreck and damaging
Dad's car. Worried I couldn't deliver
these many boys to their parents' doorsteps

in time to get the car back to the lot
at the mill where I'd promised
to pick Dad up after his shift.
Man, you're shit-faced, my brother
said to the last of his buddies
who couldn't seem to rally
from his slouch and get out of the car.

He'd been issued his draft card, my brother,
and I worried about that. I'd be draft-age in June
and I worried about that, too. Dad sniffed smoke
as soon as he'd slid in behind the wheel.
Said nothing. Wouldn't look at me. Wouldn't look
at his eldest sprawled in the backseat,
snoring and gagging and snoring more.

* Voice from sky (older brother): . . . *Let's get stupid!*
Boy looks distressed. Looks toward Narrator for help. Narrator refuses.

** Voice from sky (pals laughing): *Pussy! . . . You pussy!*
Young Man visibly winces.

*** Voice from sky (older brother): *Man, you're shit-faced!*

Father enters stage left, carrying lunch box. Sits down beside son, bumps him over, takes the wheel. Father sniffing the air. Shakes his head disapprovingly.

Snoring sounds increase as lights fade to black.

Action

Action speaks louder than words, Kenny
chided us. We'd just walked home to the dorm
from a rally on the commons,
spitting bullets at Nixon and his war.
We huddled and passed a pipe. Lit candles and aimed
a black-light at Hendrix ghosting on the wall.

Don't you just want to trash something? said Kenny.
Right-on, Ted said and raised a clenched fist:
Smash the state! Right-on, Man. The rest of us

agreed. *Love Generation rules!*
We passed the pipe again and chased it

with a three dollar bottle of Bali-Hai. Larry
went teary-eyed. *Think of it,* he said,
*It's up to us. We're like what's-his-name Jefferson,
Abe Lincoln, Man. We're . . . like making history, Man.*

Let's do it, Kenny shouted, *Do it, Man!*

"Gonna be a revolution . . . " thumped from the stereo
and we sang it loud . . . .
We're like a movement, Man, Larry said.
We're like . . . a tidal wave. We're like . . . .
Someone had sent 'round a few crumbs of hashish
flaming on a tinfoil wrapper. *We're like . . .*
but he coughed and coughed and couldn't force
another word. *You're like wasted, Man,* I said.

It's cosmic, Man, Kenny said. *Don't you see?*

It's all atoms. Everything.
All made up of atoms.
All we need is . . . like . . . unlocking that atom, Man.
Ted snored. Larry rolled himself up in a rug,
knocking an empty bottle, spinning.
The needle on the LP blipped
on the last groove over and over. Ticking like a bomb.
No, ticking like a countdown. No, ticking like a clock.

Bell — characters position themselves.
      — sound: marching feet.
      — screen: peace march, photo.

Young Man and Extras cross-legged, downstage.
Smoky dorm room.

* Kenny (Extra): *Action speaks louder than*
     words, Man . . .

Passing a joint around.

** Kenny (Extra): *. . . Don't you just want to*
     smash something, Man!
*** Ted (Extra): *. . . Right on! . . . Smash the*
     State! . . . Right on, Man!
**** Kenny, Ted, Larry (Extras): *Love*
     Generation rules! We fucking rule,
     Man!

***** Larry (Extra): *Man! Think of it, Man!*
     It's up to us. We're like what's-his-
     name Jefferson, Abe Lincoln, Man.
     We're . . . like making history, Man.

****** Kenny (Extra): *Let's do it! Do it, Man!*

Extras sing: "Gonna be a revolution . . ."

******* Larry (Extra): *We're like a*
     movement, Man. We're like . . . a tidal
     wave. We're like . . . .
******** Larry continues: *We're like . . . .*
     (coughing, gagging.)
******** Young Man (sarcastic): *You're like*
     . . . wasted, Man.
Marching feet sound turns into ticking clock.
Screen changes to stuck needle on stereo.
********* Kenny (Extra): *It's cosmic, Man.*
     Don't you see?
(Ted collapsed. Snoring.)
********* Kenny continues: *It's all atoms.*
     Everything. All made up of
     atoms. All we need is . . .
     like . . . unlocking that atom, Man.

Ticking increases in volume as lights fade to
black.

Bell — characters position themselves.
           — sound: snow blowing, dog panting.
           — screen: steadily blowing snow.

Young Man in winter coat, sitting on edge of Tier One. He's busy trying to please the invisible girl beside him. (Emphasize humor.)

Kissing

Narrator watching, bemused.

Her friend and her friend's new guy
paired up in the front seat,
already unbuttoning each other
and moaning like they were lapping cream,
while she insisted I lay the backseat down
so we could sprawl lengthwise on a blanket.

Hurry, she said, *hurry. Shut the door,*
there's snow blowing in, don't get the blanket wet.
I'd seen my dad drop the seat flat
for loads of groceries, and I did finally
— after much fumbling — figure out the latch
though I gashed my palm.

* Voice from sky (girlfriend): *Hurry . . . . Shut the door! . . . There's snow blowing in . . . don't get the blanket wet!*

(Young Man continues to struggle.)

Meanwhile in the blackness, arms and legs flailed
up front, honking accidently,
bumping open the glove box, spilling Mom's stash
of plastic picnic-ware clattering to the floor.

(Horn honk. Clattering sounds.)

Shit, shit, my girl hissed when she'd spied
my bloody palm smeared on her pink ski coat
and commenced to vigorously ridding herself
of the stain by swiping it across my sleeve.

** Voice from sky (girlfriend): *Shit, shit, shit!*

(Dog panting gets louder.)

Then, despite it all, we nuzzled lip to lip,
though she raised her head up between kisses
to sigh longingly toward the wrestling silhouettes
of her friend and her friend's new guy entwined,

(Young Man wrestling with invisible girl. Smooching noises.)

and, frankly, I worried I'd fall short
of what she might expect of me beyond the two of us
bedded side by side in coats and snowboots.
So I pressed my face up close and closer,
and like an eager Labrador pup
I nosed and tasted her, kissing and kissing more.

(Young Man visibly confused, panicked.)

Lights fade to black.

Bell — characters position themselves.
      — sound: phone. Ringing stops when
        Narrator begins.
      — screen: long scene of telephone lines.

You Don't Sound So Good

My father on the phone won't complain.
His voice strangles with phlegm.
Till I wish he'd cough and clear
the line over a thousand miles
of static between his house and mine.

Young Man, Tier Two, facing stage right (away
from Father), phone to his ear. Standing, impatient,
fidgeting.

Father in rocking chair, not rocking, head back, eyes
closed.

Now I press the earpiece against my head
on the lost chance of hearing what's gone
unsaid. *Sure, the kids are fine.*
The weather's rarely a surprise.
The talk slows. I wince

* Young Man: *Sure . . . ah huh . . . kids are doing fine.*

and listen to his throat, how the air
scrapes in, then bubbles and cracks. Till the silence
nearly kills us both. Same knot
stifled in his chest, thickens in mine.
I swallow it back. *Your mother,*

** Father: *. . . Your mother . . . won't like she's missed*
        this call . . .

he says, *won't like she's missed this call.*
I'm baffled. After all these years
I should be good at this. I should promise
I'll call back. But I don't. *You don't
sound so good,* I tell him. *Just old,*
he says. I wait and listen to his breathing.

*** Young Man: *You don't . . . sound so good . . .*
**** Father: *. . . just . . . old . . .*

You know how she is . . . he adds to hint
I'm wrong for having grown and wrong
for leaving. *I'm just old.*

***** Father: *You know how she is . . .*

****** Father: *. . . I'm just old . . . that's all . . .*

Now it's complaint.
That's all, he rasps. And again: *That's all.*

(Young Man visibly agitated.)
******* Father: *. . . That's . . . . all.* (Big sigh.)

I don't have an answer. Marvel at his restraint.
But . . . your mother . . . he stabs it home,
she won't like she's missed this call . . .

******** Father: *. . . But . . . your mother . . . she*
        won't like she's missed this call . . .

Lights fade, then brighten when bell rings.

Bell — characters position themselves.
— sound: winds blowing.
— screen: kitchen again, same as
earlier.

Young Man in rocking chair.
Father on Tier Two, pacing back and forth.
Mother looking out window, her back to everyone.

Change Finds My Hometown

Not that I mind them being here, that's not it.
Just wanna know why they drive better cars
than mine. Somebody give 'em them cars,
why don't they give me one? I worked hard
all my life and nobody give me shit.
Why these Chinese get all the favors?

* Father: *Not that I mind them being here, that's not it.*
Just wanna know why they drive better cars
than mine. Somebody give 'em them cars,
why don't they give me one? I worked hard all
my life and nobody give me shit. Why these
Chinese get all the favors?

Not Chinese, Dad, my sister says, *They're Hmong.*

** Voice from sky (adult sister): *Not Chinese, Dad. . . .*
They're Hmong.

Mom chimes in from the kitchen:
So much crime we got now. Just read the papers.
Can't feel safe nowhere. Maybe these Hmong
that come over here aren't so bad, but their kids
are mean. They got gangs beatin' up
on kids who been born here.

*** Mother: *So much crime we got now. Just read the*
papers. Can't feel safe nowhere. Maybe these
Hmong that come over here aren't so bad, but
their kids are mean . . . They got gangs beatin'
up on kids who been born here.

I'm listening
from the Easy Chair, pretending to watch TV.
My first visit home in years, and I'm stumbling
to navigate the family. *It's changed,* I say loud,
can't deny it.

**** Young Man: *It's changed . . . can't deny it.*

What did you expect,
my sister says, *the world is shifting and won't stop.*
She's right. She's up close with Hmong enrollees
in her classroom and their families after school.

***** Voice from sky (sister): *What do you expect?*
The world is shifting and won't stop.

She's big-hearted to a fault. Wants us all
to get along. It's Mom and Pop I can't figure;
they used to walk evenings up and down the block
visiting neighbors till past dark. Now they're
locked

in their own home. *It's hard,* my sister says.
You bet it's hard, Mom says and bites her lip.

****** Voice from sky (sister): *. . . It's hard . . .*
******* Mother: *. . . You bet it's hard . . .*

Yeah, Dad says with a sigh.
It's never been easy,
he says . . . *never been easy for nobody.*

******** Father: *Yeah . . . It's never been easy . . . . .*
never been easy for nobody.

Lights fade, then brighten when bell rings.

Bell — characters position themselves.
       — sound: clock ticking.
       — screen: mill smokestacks.

Father standing at window on Tier Two,
looking out.

Narrator studying Father.

Thirty-five Years

Thirty-five years at Bowman's Timber Mill
stretched thin between the rumored thrills
of maybe making foreman, or when his knees ached
and he hobbled like a gnome — maybe he'd take
the pen-and-clipboard job when the tallyman quit.
But the tallyman stayed on and nothing came of it.
Or maybe he'd work a whole new place, pick up and move
toward barroom promises of better pay,
which never seemed to prove

true. *What are you gonna do, Freddie, what now?*
Buddies at his retirement picnic wanted to glimpse how
a man's life might slip into the dreams he'd wished.
Relax in the sun and fish, he said, but I don't believe he fished
even once after that. He'd rise like clockwork at dawn,
dress in the work jeans and flannel shirts he'd worn
thousands of mornings before. Sip coffee,
cock a lonesome ear for the shift whistle and rhythms
now his bones could hear —

logs rumbling, the saw's wail, lumber tumbling
toward the bundle carts. He'd sink into silent grumbling;
What good is fetching home a stringer of bluegills
when your kids are grown and gone?
When the empty house fills
with the ghost of possibilities long past? He'd wander back
to the log yard, perch in an open car along the track,
glad to walk with his buddies, laugh and drink,
a man who knew at last what's true. *Besides,* he'd say,
fish don't bite like they used to.

* Voice from sky (work buddies): . . . *What*
       are you gonna do, Freddie, what
       now?
** Father startled . . . looks up toward
voice.

Father turns to address audience.

*** Father: *What good is fetching home*
       a stringer of bluegills when your
       kids are grown and gone?

(Father turns to look at mill on screen.)

**** Father: *Besides . . . fish don't bite . . .*
       like they used to.

Lights fade, then brighten when bell rings.

Bell — characters position themselves.
　　　— sound: muffled heartbeat.
　　　— screen: country kitchen again.

Mother walks on and off stage left, bringing
boxes she sets on the edge of Tier One. She
opens boxes, begins sorting, inspecting.
(Emphasize humor.)

Narrator studying her.

Young Man looking in from behind window.

Sentimental Value

Our mother, as family archivist, took it upon herself
to collect her children's assorted artifacts,
whatever odd scraps marked our material selves.
And she accumulated stacks of storage boxes, hoping
we'd hallow these family mementos
and prize the tenacity of our mother's intentions
to hand down to the rest of us what she couldn't let go.

Crude scribbles of crayon and grade school worksheets
stiff with glue. Birthday cards and Valentine hearts,
pages and pages of wide-ruled penmanship
practiced in soft lead. Smudged mimeographed
school pageant programs listing our names
for thirty seconds of recitative fame. Grade reports
of average merit. Third-place ribbons. Honorable mentions
with no mention of which particular honors we'd
almost accomplished. These histories multiplied

and piled precariously toward collapse. One wet spring
the boxes moldered, and our mother painstakingly
sorted the wreckage and salvaged all she could.
Her children, of course, eventually begat
families of their own, and when we'd visit she'd unearth
the archives and offer . . . *Take away whatever you want.*

Later she said, *Please take it. Please!*

Haven't you heard, we'd joke,
you can't take it with you?

Fine, she'd reply, *but how'd I get stuck with it
all this time between?* We did, in later years, enjoy
scattered moments unpacking our distant past,
while our mother sat nearby and smiled, guiding us
authoritatively, appraising remnants we might
otherwise have mistakenly burned as trash.

* Mother (horrified.): *Aarrgghh!*

** Mother (to audience): *Take away whatever
　　you want . . .*
*** Mother: *Please take it . . . . please!*

**** Young Man (looking in from behind
window, joking): *Haven't you heard?. . . You
　　can't take it with you!*
***** Mother (petulant): *Fine! . . . But
　　how'd I get stuck with it all this time
　　between?*

Boxes remain on Tier One.

Lights remain bright.

Bell — characters position themselves.
       — sound: clock ticking.
       — screen: country kitchen again.

Mother sitting on edge of Tier Two, pencil and notebook in hand.

Father in rocking chair, reading newspaper.

Young Man looking in from behind window. Narrator, studying them all.

Someone Needs to Keep Track

We'd been tucked into bed, my brothers and I,
and the house had fallen silent accordingly.
I'd hear my mother call out in a half-whisper
from the kitchen table to my father in an adjacent room.
He'd be unfolding his newspaper and settling in his chair.
How much were groceries? Mom said.
Twenty something, Dad said back.
How much exactly, Mom insisted.

    * Mother: *How much were groceries?*
    ** Father: *Twenty something.*

    *** Mother: *How much exactly?*

The springs in Dad's recliner creaked
as he reached for his wallet, and I pictured him
thumbing a thin wad of cash. *Twenty-seven,* he'd say
Then a pause in which the hallway clock kept tocking.
And change? she'd ask.
Forty-five, he'd say. *No, fifty-five.*

    **** Father: *Twenty-seven.*

    ***** Mother: *. . . And change? . . .*
    ****** Father: *Forty-five . . . No, fifty-five.*

This was the nightly ritual,
Mom's accounting — a page a day — in her record book.
She listed every cent ever spent.
How cold was it this morning? she'd ask.

    ******* Mother: *How cold was it this morning?*

Below zero, he'd reply.
Are you sure? she'd push.

    ******** Father: *Below zero.*
    ********* Mother: *Are you sure? . . .*

Damn sure, he'd say.
Nearly froze my nose off.

    ********** Father: *Damn sure . . . . Nearly froze my nose off.*

She'd jot that down, too,
the below zero part, but nothing about Dad's nose.
And nothing much about the rest of us, either.
Except who stayed home from school sick that day,
who needed new Sunday shoes, which of us
got his hair cut, which forgot his coat on the bus.

Not so much as a single syllable she'd pen
to let us know who she was beyond these pages.
We grew up. Mom withered into her grave. Her yearly
statistics lived on, ranked in a dusty row, a forgotten closet
where we could dig up the facts, if we wanted.
A catalog of seasonal temperature changes,
the rising costs of milk and bread and cheese.

Mother quietly exits upstage via steps behind Tier Two.

Clock stops ticking.
Father stops rocking. Freezes.

Lights go black, suddenly.

Bell — characters position themselves.
    — sound: none.
    — screen: black night, stars.

Young Man sitting on Tier One, pillow in hand.

Invisible Shrink in rocking chair.

Narrator on his knees, observing nearby.

The Pillow

He handed me a pillow,
a little upholstered couch-cushion pillow.
It's your mother, he said.
Tell her what you've wanted to tell her.
All of it. The pillow was worn bare
in spots and stained.

* Voice from sky (Shrink): *It's your mother . . . tell her what you've wanted to tell her. . . . All of it.*

Young Man looks at rocking chair, confused.

Okay, Ma, I droned, *how's it going?*
The pillow said nothing back.
You can do it, he said. *Tell her.*
He stared at me. I stared
at the pillow. *Tell her what?* I asked,
surprised my voice cracked.
A jagged shard of anger.

** Young Man (addressing pillow): *. . . Okay, Ma . . . how's it going?*
*** Voice from sky: *You can do it! Tell her. . .*

**** Young Man (agitated): *. . . Tell her what? . . .*

Ah, he said. *You want to make a fist and hit her?* He leaned forward,
coaching me to go on, pleased
this discomfort proved itself
worth two hundred bucks an hour.

\.

***** Voice from sky: *Ah . . . You want to make a fist and hit her? . . .*

The little pillow looked sad. And tired.
I felt sad and tired. She'd wanted
just a piece of what she'd dreamt of
as a girl. A thimbleful of something
more than daily chores afforded.
Not much of a pillow, really,
but not a bad pillow.

I stood and shoved the pillow back.
The way I was raised, I said . . .
never hit a girl . . . most especially your mother.
I'd failed to break down like he'd wanted.
Failed him — his opportunity to display compassion,
a man-hug to comfort some poor slob sobbing . . . .

(Young Man throws pillow at rocking chair.)
****** Young Man: *The way I was raised . . . never hit a girl . . . especially your mother!*

Wasn't much, me and that pillow.
But it felt like something right
to defend her. To let the sad pillow be.
To not lay easy blame on her. To know
she and I survived our disappointments.
To know I'd loved her all along.

(Narrator and Young Man lock meaningful, united glances.)

Lights fade to black.

Bell — characters position themselves.
        — sound: none.
        — screen: black night, stars.

Young Man stands near tombstone. Narrator stands close behind him.

Young Man narrates.

Ghosting Home

In his final years, my father's frame
shrunk, while his wardrobe stayed the same.
Where once his belly might have overlapped
beleaguered belt loops of his stain-dappled
pants, now he'd contracted inches enough
the waistband gapped. Shoulders of his rough
denim work shirts outsized him day-by-day,
his shoes so loose they threatened to walk away

without him. I could hardly stomach the pace
of his diminishing size; but, in truth, his face . . .
well, I couldn't face him. That spooked look
magnified behind thick-rimmed lenses. The hook
of his nose chiseled narrow as a blade.
His mouth gaped open, quivering and afraid,
the jaw slackened till the lips rounded
the relentless *oh-oh-oh* of a soul astounded

        * Voice from sky (weakly): . . . *oh, oh, oh* . . .

by his own decline. My siblings lived nearby
and tenderly, bravely nursed him. And I
lived an insulated two days' drive apart from the past,
I thought, but duty or guilt brought me back.
Or was it love? I wanted to ask him but lost

        ** Narrator (Old Man): . . . *Or was it love?* . . .

the chance, though I said it anyway as I tossed
a handful of dust on his coffin. And turned to go.

And drove home slowly, knowing what I know.

Young Man and Narrator embrace awkwardly.

Young Man exits upstage via steps behind Tier Two.

Lights fade, then brighten. No bell.

Bell — none.
         — sound: faint ocean waves.
         — screen: Oregon beach photo.

Narrator in rocking chair. Manuscript on his lap. He's studying something small in his hand. He positions rocking chair to face audience.

Boy enters from stage right. Drapes blanket around Narrator's shoulders. Sits cross-legged at Narrator's feet. Narrator addresses Boy.

Listening

A pebble caught in my shoe
troubles my progress
halts me on a precipice
along a well-worn path overlooking the surf.

I sit in tall grass,
undo laces,
lift the pebble
between my thumb and forefinger.

And I ask what it has to say,
solitary inaudible squeak
lost in the grand mashing
of tides pounding the shoreline.

But did I mention
today is my sixtieth birthday?
Three score orbits
on a big rock in the black empty.

                                          * Boy (congratulatory): *Your birthday!*

Well . . . not such a big rock really
— a pebble —
in comparison to our daystar,
even less to larger lights in the night sky . . . .

I pocket this quiet stone home
and sit with it in my palm late tonight,
listening. Listening
to the winds pummeling the dunes
and the relentless ocean grinding.

Boy rises. Narrator hands over manuscript. Boy and Narrator, forehead to forehead. Pause.

Lights go black, suddenly.

(Act Two closes with chorus to "Hey Jude.")

Lights return.

Characters come out dancing joyously. Bow.

Poet's Notes:

36 Essays for Reflection and Discussion

Poet's Notes: Some Memories Never Leave

My poems tell stories. People ask, "Did that really happen?" I've learned to answer like this: "It's all true; some of it is even fact." That's a little joke, of course. The content of my poems are 80 percent autobiographical, 80 percent stories I've made up, and 80 percent I can't discern whether I've made them up or not. That's the trigonometry of poetry. Psychologists call it "confabulation." We perceive experience subjectively, often inaccurately. We color experience through the warped lens of our emotions, our biases, our blind spots. Two people in the same room witnessing the same event can interpret the "facts" of the situation very differently. That's why, when my siblings and I sit down to reminisce, we discover we've lived side-by-side in different worlds — same parents, same address, same era, but more or less each of us has invented what we call "memories."

I'm a storyteller, and I'm conscious that my narratives morph over time. My wife used to object to this. "That's not how you said it happened last time you told it," she'd say. She's since learned to tolerate my factual inconsistencies. Maybe people in general (me, too) want to believe we see and experience the world accurately. Stability and predictability offer us a sense of security, and who doesn't want that? But the art of storytelling feeds on the freedom that comes from letting the particulars of the story shift and reshape themselves over time. It's a lot like reclining in a hammock and watching the clouds billow into what looks like a pirate ship one moment and then a spaceship the next. Here's a story I love to tell: My son, Aamon, and I were camping on an island in Flathead Lake, and we decided to pack up and head for shore in the middle of the night because the mosquitoes were killing us. Aamon lay on his back in the boat, looking up at the blackness and the stars. "Oh . . . there's Moby Dick," he mused. "No . . . no, that star moved . . . so make that . . . Moby Duck!" He's got the hang of it — children are good at letting the imagination outwit reality.

I said in the paragraph above that storytelling relied on letting the particulars reshape "themselves." Lots of writers have mentioned this — the necessity to step aside and let the poem or story lead the way. The particulars will shape themselves in surprising and inventive ways if only our artist-egos will let go. It's as if the story wants a life of its own, wants volition and agency. Artistic freedom, therefore, means both the artist and the art object itself crave the flexibility to stretch and reinvent themselves. "My poems tell stories," I said in the very first line of this essay. I mean that literally. Well, 80 percent literally and 80 percent figuratively.

In the poem "Some Memories Never Leave," the speaker of the poem — a very young child — is both falling asleep and waking to his innermost self on a warm summer evening with the windows wide and curtains lifting and falling in the twilight breeze. His father and a neighbor, both mill laborers, have stolen for themselves an evening of fun, clinking beers and blowing on a trombone, inventing bluesy expressions of joy and sorrow. "This becomes the music of my heart," says the child. Now, he's the fledgling poet, feeling his own blood linked in the chain of human connections. He's begun to marvel at a rudimentary puzzle of existence: We are cast into this world mysteriously, inextricably enmeshed in circumstances which brought us here in the first place. What are we to make of the situation we've been given? This is how the story opens, mine . . . and yours, too. How will it unfold?

Poet's Notes: Buzz-Cut Saturdays

Our home felt empty whenever Dad wasn't there. He'd leave for work early in the morning while his kids were still sleeping. Mom would pack his lunchbox, and in the dim light of each new day, he'd set out walking along the railroad tracks toward his job at the lumber mill. We could hear the shift whistles sounding, and when we heard the closing whistle in the evening, we knew Dad would be home soon. On weekends, he'd be with us all day. This was the rhythm of our lives.

Even just a few years ago, if you'd asked me to recount the "story" of my life, I'd have listed a chronology of mileposts, the big events that shaped me — learning to read, learning to swim, a first crush and first kiss, first car and first solo cross-country drive. Also funerals and marriages and graduations. Now, as an older person, I glimpse how painfully easy it's been to overlook the significance of mundane daily chores and rituals. I've taken so much for granted. Don't we all? I've been a sleepwalker most of my days, waiting for something important to happen, and all the while my eyes were closed to the miraculous gift of ordinary days. "Life is what happens," said John Lennon, "while you are busy making other plans."

I've heard that some combat soldiers find civilian life too plain, too much of nothing happening. My father wasn't like that. He was a World War II vet, but he longed for peace and quiet, camaraderie, a garden, long afternoons in a lawn chair along the river watching for fish to nibble and pull the bobber under. He'd been a gunner in Patton's army. He seldom spoke of it. We'd ask, and he'd wrinkle his brow as if he could hardly recall. A person can be blind to the ordinary; a person also can be blinded by things too horrible to stare at directly.

Still, Dad never forgot the war, and his metaphor of "the good soldier" became his go-to guide for how a man should comport himself, the most important lessons he knew to pass along to his sons. The mythical hero-soldier especially — the selfless comrade who braves enemy fire to rescue the wounded — Dad used over and again as a touchstone for his kids to hold in mind. Our pains were nothing in comparison, and we shouldn't whine. This "tough it out" or "man up" attitude is now a mostly outdated measure of masculinity; let's thank the passage of time for that. Men and boys now are allowed feel what they feel. Some of us will even dare to cry.

So Dad sat us down on a tall stool in the middle of the kitchen floor, wrapped a dish towel around our shoulders, and shaved our heads like we were new recruits. Assembly-line style, my brothers and I took a turn in the chair, letting Dad's electric clippers groom our scalps like a lawnmower shearing grass. The "flat-top" was in fashion back then, but Dad wasn't much into fashion. His way was to punctuate our craniums with a few nicks and scrapes and to shave us almost bald.

Is it easy to know when someone loves you? Or not? My father wouldn't or couldn't offer hugs and kisses. Sure felt comforting, though, to feel his calloused hands cupping my chin to hold me from squirming.

44

Poet's Notes: Bull-Headed

Montana poet Richard Hugo wrote with reverence about alders and catfish. Literary scholars and critics contend that, for Hugo, alders and catfish are symbols of stubborn persistence and resilience in face of adversity. That could be true and probably is . . . but I know as a poet, I'm not consciously in the business of loading my poems with figurative literary devices, and I bet Hugo would say the same.

Another Montana writer, William Kittredge, talks about the "generative and associative" powers of language. In the act of putting the pen to the page, experienced writers relish moments of unexpected joy when they discover themselves saying surprisingly wonderful things, as if language itself has taken over to generate thoughts more beautiful and brilliant than we might come upon alone. Can it be, through language, a writer may connect to what Carl Jung called "the collective unconscious"? That's how it feels, on a good day, when I've arrived at the bottom of the page: What I've written feels like so much more than me. It's as if the words themselves have carried me into unexpected heights of transcendence in which I'm the humble mouthpiece for the larger voice — the collective unconscious — of all humanity. This feels especially strange when I'm writing about what seems to be my own small experience in the world, which is how I begin most of my poems.

How can I write about my own experience and still be speaking for the collective experience of my species? Well, that's a long and complicated conversation. Let's put our heads together over a cup of hot brew someday and see where our talking takes us. I suspect the answer is this: If we go deep enough into our own lives, we discover that our fundamental experience in this world is pretty much the same as everyone else's. That's a good notion for a writer to keep in mind, and it can serve as a defense against becoming too self-involved. Our own mundane lives are just that — unremarkable, nothing special. Paradoxically, our own mundane lives are also luminous portraits of the "human condition." My face is yours, and your face is mine.

We do a disservice to students and other readers in perpetuating the notion that writers hide meaning inside complex tropes and that scholarly analysis is the only way to appreciate and understand a poem. The Billy Collins poem "Introduction to Poetry" humorously complains that too often we want to tie a poem to the chair and beat the meaning out of it with a rubber hose. That poem, too, is loaded with symbols, pretty strong ones, but first and foremost Billy Collins just wants us to laugh.

I'll venture a guess that Hugo wrote about alders and catfish because they fascinated him, caught his imagination. He recognized their unacknowledged magnificence, and he wanted us to do the same. A critic could make lots of deep psychological suppositions about my poem "Bull-Headed." Is it a poem about a son in awe of his father? Or does the poem want the reader to philosophize upon the hidden inner workings of the wild? Or is it a poem simply and directly about a fish . . . and a boy's fascination to look upon a heap of guts and see a real heart still throbbing?

It's a praise poem, I think.

Poet's Notes: Working on My Words

People ask, "When did you start writing?" Some writers start relatively late in life; some start early. I claim to have entered the writing profession before I started school. I couldn't read yet, but I remember being thrilled with the alphabet, all those shapes, each a little message on its own, symbols with sounds. I remember scanning the alphabet in my mind to compose a message: I C U or Y B U? Well, that's ridiculous, of course, but I concentrated on that project for long afternoons, determined to crack the code.

My older brother went off to school before I did; I was proud of him, and I was filled with envy. Then he came home with books, and he'd learned to read. This was an earthquake in my brain. I remember looking over his shoulder as he pointed to words and pronounced them. Again I felt proud of him, but now I was also insanely jealous. I hatched a plan: I'd snatch his books whenever he was busy elsewhere. I'd hide away in a far corner of a closet with a flashlight and a tablet . . . and I'd copy the words I'd heard him read. The flimsy, saddle-stitched texts told tales of two kids my age, Alice and Jerry, and their frisky dog, Jip. "Run, Jip, run!" "See the ball?" "Run, jump, play." I'm not sure how, but I figured it out. I called it "working on my words." I launched my career as a writer right then and there, one big block letter at a time.

So . . . I began as a closet writer, but there's a more important point I'd like to make at this juncture. Some people experience early in life an eerie awakening to the fact of their own existence. Elizabeth Bishop's poem "In The Waiting Room" describes with grace and precision this moment of nascent existential consciousness. The speaker of the poem, a young girl, is reading *National Geographic* magazines in the waiting room of a dentist's office. She's only six years old; she's journeyed there with her aunt, who is receiving treatment in a room nearby. This was 1918, and the magazines are filled with grotesque images of nearly naked exotic tribes, their "awful hanging breasts," and their necks wound round with wire "like necks of a lightbulb." Suddenly, the young girl hears her aunt cry out, or at least she thinks it's her aunt's cry. "What took me / completely by surprise / was that it was me: / my voice, in my mouth," the girl says. She is shaken, having awakened to the fact of her own existence: "But I felt; you are an I, / you are an 'Elizabeth,' / you are one of them." I used the word "eerie" to describe this awakening as I experienced it; Bishop uses the word "unlikely." "How — I didn't know any / word for it — how 'unlikely' . . . / How had I come to be here, like them . . . ?"

That's what I felt while I waited with my father for his mother to die. I was conscious that night of being "one of them," a living being, sprung from a long line of those who'd walked on this earth before me. Just as my grandmother was passing, my soul entered my body, and my life's path opened before me. Words are my work. I discovered my calling early on.

When did you discover your calling? Tell me, please, when did this happen for you?

Poet's Notes: She Didn't Like What She Didn't Know

Taste, touch, smell, hearing, sight. Gustatory, tactile, olfactory, auditory, visual. Five senses. Or are there more? How about our sense of time? Sense of humor? Sense of direction? Sense of belonging? How about empathy? Isn't that a kind of sensing? When we walk into a room, we can "feel the tension in the air." What sort of sense is that, a barometer to gauge the emotional climate in a room? Posture, gesture, facial expression — all send messages. The pace, volume, and inflection of language can tell us a lot, too. Eavesdropping on two people talking in the next room, we can hear the emotional temperature of the conversation — too hot, too cold, and degrees between. How do we do that?

People have antennae, and I think they are big long ones. Like the cockroach, we move forward with our antennae sensing, reading, and absorbing information beyond our five senses. I say this in the classroom, and students think I'm joking. Well . . . 80 percent I am, 80 percent I'm not. As a culture, we value what we can taste, touch, see, here, smell . . . and we we mistrust and devalue our intuitive senses. Yes, sometimes we "have a hunch," and we are wrong. On the other hand, sometimes we have a hunch, and we are dead right. Scientific experimentation begins with hunches or hypotheses, some eventually proven right, some wrong. We're pretty sure of some things, but we're pretty much just guessing at a lot more. Science depends on objective, empirical, rational thought, but it's often the "Eureka!" moment of intuitive insight which opens the door and reveals the pathway to further research.

I mention all this because, as a poet and as a person, I rely heavily on hunches and intuition. I think it's a personality trait common in artists. I'm in love with the five physical senses, but I'm amorous toward all their nonphysical sister senses, too. Writing teachers recommend we stay grounded in the physical realm by putting lots of sensory information into our poems. That's good advice. "No ideas but in things," said William Carlos Williams. In his poem "The Red Wheelbarrow," he gives us just that, a wheelbarrow. In bringing us face to face with an object, he nudges us to look hard and see beyond the object. The wheelbarrow is speaking tons of abstractions, ideas, meanings. We see and touch the wheelbarrow, and those sensory cues stimulate our brains into shaping abstract meaning. It doesn't work the other way around; ideas and abstraction will not stimulate us to see and touch a wheelbarrow. At least that's the way it seems to be. That's my hunch.

In the poem "She Didn't Like What She Didn't Know," I'm a child learning how to operate and read my antennae. I see and hear my parents, their tone of voice, their gestures. My antennae register more than my eyes' limited vision. My antennae see little ripples in the air when Mom and Dad pass by one another self-consciously. My antennae sense moods gathering like a storm. My antennae feel blood pressure building toward thunder.

Oh, my dear antennae. I've had a long love-hate relationship with my big cockroach antennae. One kid or another must wear in his heart what's broken and unspoken between his parents. Often, it's the middle kid, and I was one of those. It's painful for me to remember even now, though as an adult I clearly see how I would have been accurately labeled an "overly sensitive" child. I couldn't stop those antennae from poking into places they shouldn't have been buzzing around. Oh, my dear antennae. I want also to praise and thank my antennae. Clearly, I wouldn't know how to look for poems without them.

Poet's Notes: "Bath Time!"

Was your childhood joyous? Was it tragic? I'd guess it was a combination of both, like mine. So much depends upon how we choose to tell the story. Over time, we color our memories to suit the identity we've chosen. And memories degrade, year by year, until we can't clearly recall how we've embellished and twisted our history or how we've forever knotted together fact and fiction. As a poet, I don't worry about these things; I'm inventing my life inwardly and outwardly as I walk along. Doesn't everyone? I wouldn't want a perfectly happy childhood or a perfectly rotten and painful one either. I'd be robbing myself of the rainbow by painting my experience merely a single color.

Once, I met a troubled young man who'd survived a surreal and tragic childhood. I was working as an counselor to disadvantaged college students, and this young man spent many hours in front of my desk, telling me his tale. He'd been more or less imprisoned in a high-rise apartment overlooking a bustling Chicago neighborhood. He lived alone with his mother, and she would beat him if he moved too near the door. She suffered a catalog of disorders and addictions. He could see people on the street below, but they were too distant to read their faces. He could see children milling in the school playground, but he couldn't hear their voices. This went on for years.

At night, after his mother passed out, he'd turn on the TV and watch *The Johnny Carson Show.* Mostly he kept the sound off, lest he rouse his mother's wrath. He was fascinated to witness people laughing, how their faces changed, how their eyes lit with joy. He told me about Johnny Carson because I'd asked him what he might like to do for a career. He wanted to be Johnny Carson; he wanted to make people laugh. He'd practice his jokes on me. In the midst of his misery, he'd unearthed his heart's desire.

I was scruffy and ragged as a kid, and so were my siblings. We knew families who owned two cars and lived in bigger houses than ours, but we knew families who were scraping by, meal to meal, and paying rent. Rich or poor, some were happy, some not. I found my happiness like the kid watching Johnny Carson. I convulsed with terror whenever my parents quarreled, but on a good day, I felt rich and loved. I had a wealth of freedom; this was my good fortune. We lived at the edge of town, a sort of no-man's land, not farmland but not city yet either, just vistas of empty fields and forests to explore. I spent whole summers half-naked, hip-deep in duckweed swamps. We slid on our butts down the muddy creek banks, like otters. We didn't have a lot of rules because our parents were occupied making ends meet and puzzling out how to stay married. Hungry mosquitoes feasted on our necks. Leeches sucked blood from our ankles. We ran in the trees, howling like happy wolves.

Poet's Notes: Washday, Everyday

What stirs inside us when we dream of something better, more fulfilling, than what we have now? Aspirations can bring us good fortune, and aspirations can cause us pain. Our waking dreams might needle us toward risking the effort to make them real. Our waking dreams might also simply be an escape from drudgery, a salve to cover the soreness of loneliness and discontent. A psychologist once told me that there are two kinds of dreamers — dreamers who implement small steps, day by day, toward bringing their aspirations to light, and dreamers who sit with their aspirations idly, wallowing in their imaginations like elephants in a mud-bath.

Look around — the walls of our world are pasted full of inspirational posters admonishing timidity, advocating that we should "dare to dream." Bookshelves are lined with titles telling us how to make our lives more fulfilling, how to move away from what we have now . . . toward something better elsewhere. Easier said than done. For so many of us, dreams are the tomorrow we hope to wake in, while today is only a waiting room where we've fallen asleep, and over and over the train departs without us. I dream to accomplish next year what I've failed to accomplish the year before. The future arrives, and I'm empty-handed, still napping. We dream a new dream to push the future forward, to keep tomorrow at arm's length, a carrot on a stick, propelling us to plod ever onward, reaching toward what maybe we're half-hoping will elude us always.

This sounds awfully dark, doesn't it? Think for a moment of someone in your life who walks about contented with their lot, at peace with the day at hand. Be careful . . . contentment can be the mask of resignation. "I'm resigned to my life as it is," some people say. This is not at all the same as someone who has accepted their station willingly, not at all like someone who lives each moment with gusto. I'd guess worldwide there's only a busload of truly contented people, mostly gurus and mystics.

As a young man leaving home for college, I accidentally unearthed a startling photo of my mother, a black-and-white snapshot tucked deep in an old trunk of mementos. She was younger than I'd ever known or imagined her to be, dressed fashionably, a dash of mischief in her eyes, one leg lifted to the running board of a sleek black Cadillac, skirt lifted rakishly to the knee. This was my mother dreaming Bonnie and Clyde — the same girl who would marry her only boyfriend (as far as I know), a boy who lived two doors down the block. The boy would go to war, and she'd send him love notes and packages. She once tried to ship him a puppy via the interstate bus lines to his basic training in Texas. He'd return from combat, they'd marry, they'd have five kids, and maybe nothing very extraordinary happened after that.

Your parents, what did they dream? And you, what is your dream? Will your children ever know your grandest, most secret plan? "Whatever you can do or dream you can, begin it; / Boldness has genius, power, and magic in it." That's from Goethe. "We are the music makers, / And we are the dreamers of dreams." That's Arthur O'Shaunessy. Obviously, these poets never cooked and cleaned for a mill-worker husband and five kids on a tight budget in the depths of winter. If my hard-laboring mother could have caught her breath long enough to confess her dreams, I imagine she'd have said something like this: "All I want is an hour to put my aching feet up and read my *Modern Romance* magazine. Or . . . a bubble bath with no children calling out for me would be nice." But she soldiered on because she had hungry mouths depending on her.

Here's another poet, William Ernest Henley: "I am the master of my fate, / I am the captain of my soul." My mother would have cast a blank look at those pretty words, shook her head, picked up her broom, and resumed her chores.

Poet's Notes: Seim's Bottle Gas

As a middle child, I felt lonely, invisible amidst our busy household with parents consumed in a constant struggle to keep the family intact. "He's a ghost," my mother would joke as I'd float room to room like a noiseless breeze, or when she'd discover me snugged in a corner, reading. But when I'd spend time with my father, just me and him, I felt less ghostly, and I have precious few memories of moments like these. Loneliness shaped me to be who I am today, a man who holds more precious than gold the rare instances when two lives surmount disconnection, when two souls bump up against one another unexpectedly, when circumstance opens our eyes, when love pours into our hearts.

"Seim's Bottle Gas" is a portrait of my father that I wouldn't have been able to write if I hadn't had the good fortune to spend some time with him devoid of all the usual family distractions. Dad took a job delivering propane, which is what we called "bottle gas" back then. It was a job between jobs, just something temporary until the union could place him elsewhere. One early summer day, he detoured from his delivery route and stopped at home. He asked, off-handedly, if I wanted to ride along. I remember climbing up into the big truck so thrilled I could hardly breathe. I felt chosen, an honor above all honors, to ride off with my father, just the two of us lumbering along. "Can I ride shotgun?" I asked over and over that summer.

We rode with the windows wide, radio blasting and my father singing along. I watched my father's lips and brow shaping the emotions of the song. Love songs lit the cab with a mid-morning deep blue sky, and troubled songs darkened around us as if storm clouds had enshrouded the sun. I was learning early lessons in poetry — though I didn't know it then — how words could whelm a person, fill his chest with sadness, or lift his fancy to fly.

So, too, I watched my father making small talk with the farmers and their wives. He was good at that, an expert smiler, an enthusiastic hand-shaker. And he was a bit of a psychologist, my father, reading what went unsaid and adjusting his words to win a man's trust. We'd be driving away from a farmer who'd just given us a wedge of cheese and a more-than-thorough tour of his barn. "I don't think he can pay," Dad would say to me, leaning in like it was our secret. "He's a nice man, but he's going broke." Or, "That's one unhappy hayseed," he'd say. "Looks like he and his wife don't mix much." These were my first lessons in deciphering the human heart and the frailties of reason and passion. Ask me, "What do you write about?" I'll answer, "People. I write about people."

Best of all, I saw sides of my father he never revealed at home. He could flirt; I don't know how far he'd carry that, but he'd smile and women smiled back. He could calculate how to get away with driving slow or stopping for a cold beer and still justify ending the day with his route unfinished. I learned that my father had dreams to be more than what he was. I learned he carried a worrisome burden, night and day, fearing he'd fail to provide for his family. He taught me what it means to be human. And humane.

Poet's Notes: Slugs (1963)

William James, American philosopher, wrote: "The greatest discovery of my generation is that human beings can alter their lives by altering their attitude of mind." That's worth thinking about. What attitudes have you held which hobbled your progress in life? What changes of attitude have helped propel you forward?

I wrote the poem "Slugs" mostly to tell the story of how, as kids, we used the little nickel-size knockouts from outlet boxes as counterfeit coins. I'm striking a humorous tone. Yet, as I recounted my tale, I realized the poem was about more than what I'd intended. It was about attitudes of mind and how my young, impressionable head had been programmed by my father. When I was very small, I stood in awe of my father as if he were a minor god. I grew beyond that, of course; by the time I was a teen, my father had shrunk to the size of an ordinary mortal. Still, the mindset my father passed on to me lingered into adulthood, and I stumble upon remnants of his philosophy stuck in back closets and dimly lit halls of my thinking even today. He was who he was, and I doubt he consciously worked to brainwash me one way or another. But I was who I was, in love with ideas at an early age, and I inhaled my father's outlook on the world whether he'd have wanted it or not.

We lived at the edge of town, and our little house looked into open fields and stands of pine. Then the town expanded, and we were suddenly surrounded by homes of strangers. We felt run-over, pushed out, shoved aside. The society we'd fit ourselves into — Dad's union buddies and their families — year by year diminished in size. Now, our town proudly advertised itself as headquarters for an insurance giant, and this meant jobs for lots of men in white shirts and ties — "rich bastards," my father called them. I doubt they were rich, but they were different. They didn't speak our grammar-be-damned language. They had carpets and TVs. They expected you to take your shoes off in the house. They polished their cars on weekends and manicured their lawns. My father resented the intruders but was helpless to stop the invasion. We weren't poor, exactly, but in comparison to our new neighbors, we felt like we had less than before.

What attitudes of mind did I glean from my father? I learned to view myself as an outsider in my own land, and I believed I should feel wounded accordingly. As a card-carrying victim of economic circumstance, I could self-righteously justify petty crimes. That's two things I learned which hobbled my progress into adulthood. I could list more, but no doubt you register my drift. Nobody was better than us, my father insisted — protesting o'er much — but it was obvious to me that our new neighbors were in a class above us, and often we looked undeniably shabby beside them.

"If you change your mind, you can change your life." These words are a continuation of the James quote above. I could say changing one's mind is like dressing in a clean shirt and shiny new suit and tie. But that metaphor isn't tailored to who I am. I'll say this: It's arduous labor indeed to pry loose outdated frames of mind and to reconstruct the foundations of thought. I'm sixty-seven years old and still hammering at it. That's a metaphor fit for my father's son.

Poet's Notes: You Be Good

Why do parents feel compelled to give their kids advice? I'm trying to recall what advice I gave to my own kids, but I'm not coming up with much worthwhile. Parents don't like to see their offspring suffer, so we issue platitudes to curb the pain, theirs and ours. We peel bandages and stick them to scraped knees, and we use words like salve to heal hurt feelings. My father had a particular brand of snake oil he favored for all fixes, a yellow salve which smelled like turpentine. "Put a little of this on it," he'd say for insect bites, for sore muscles, for warts, and for all maladies between. Then he'd give us a little lecture: "It will be okay. Don't worry. You'll be fine. It'll all work out." Once, I came home from the public pool with a couple chips of blue paint embedded deep in my foot. "Put a little of this on it," Dad said. Next morning, I had a mysterious swollen red line running from the wound to my thigh. I went swimming as usual. The red line had nearly reached my groin by then, which alerted the pool manager's attention. He called my father and persuaded him I needed more than salve. It was blood poisoning. Thank God the pool manager was a local teacher; my parents respected teachers. Had he been a lawyer or banker, I'd have been dead by the next sunrise.

"What you need," I heard my father say time and again, "is a job." Jobs kept people occupied, so they had no time to savor misery or pain. My father longed for emotional tranquility, and his stomach twisted when he witnessed people suffering. You tell me how he survived an enlistment as a machine-gunner in Patton's army. He must have seen a shit-show of horrors. Then he came home struggling to convince himself — *It will be okay. Don't worry. You'll be fine. It'll all work out.* In this manner his job became his savior, a blesséd distraction. He was elected union leader, and he managed a full platoon of workmates, buddies who relied on him for advice and guidance, fellow vets who drank to drown the war still flaming in their brains. Union summer family picnics were soaked in kegs of beer, angry bluster, and bloodied noses; like my dad, my gut churned when people didn't get along. My father rose from our picnic lunch to referee. This was expected of him. I hated it. And I was also whelmed with pride that he was my father, not one of the brawling, broken-toothed booze hounds. "You got family to think about," he'd say to an inebriated comrade, while slapping him sober. "You got work to do in the morning."

Did he persuade people? Did he change them? Did he move them and help them? Or was he protecting himself, maintaining civility so as not to rouse memories of savage devastation? What a puzzle of a man! Maybe most of all I learned from him the art of brushing aside wounds and grievances in favor of marching forward. "Just keep going," I've said to my own children. "Keep moving forward," I've advised my wife in times of turbulence. No doubt that's denial. That's just stuffing the pain. That's just holding the snake back with a long stick. No doubt that's one hard-earned strategy through the swamps of despair and self-pity.

Once, my father gifted to me a knife he'd "taken off a dead Hungarian." To this day, I'm not sure what that means. The knife handle was handcrafted, the sheath was hand laced and knotted. I'd begged him for it for years. One Sunday morning after church, he finally handed it over to me. Even then he was reluctant to let me pull it from him, and it felt like I was stealing from the dead. I carried that knife into many campsites. I kept moving forward. My son owns it now, along with the tales of his grandfather's war. We pass these things on to the next generation, and the next.

Poet's Notes: "Holy Cow!"

What's a "swear" word? Who decides? Why do we care? I was born and raised in dairy farm country — north-central Wisconsin, pastures everywhere and complacent black-and-white Holstein cows munching on the green buffet. "Holy cow!" was our favorite exclamation, and we used it dawn to dusk and sometimes mumbled it in our sleep, too. Our mothers and fathers and Sunday School teachers forbid us to "take the Lord's name in vain," so we improvised swear words to punctuate our arguments and insults. *Holy cow,* we'd say, *you're cheating! Gol darn it,* we'd spit, *that's not fair!* If the cows overheard us, they didn't give a damn. I mean, darn.

I love to eavesdrop on other people's conversations. In some ways, that's a poet's job; we've been gifted with ears wide and hungry for language in all its uses and misuses, in all its versions and perversions. Walt Whitman, bless his soul, enjoyed walking the streets of Manhattan with an eager ear cocked to the wondrous variety and inventiveness of ordinary speech. He heard poetry in that. The "chuff" of the hand, he wrote, the "blab" of the pave. These words he picked up while loitering near the loading docks, while riding street cars, while downing a mug at the pub. During his lifetime, Whitman's poems went largely unread because his poems seemed crude and prosaic in comparison to his contemporaries who employed a more formal and accepted vernacular. Today, Whitman's only book, *Leaves of Grass,* is loved across the globe. His poems are alive with the living pulse of language. Also, many scholars call Whitman the "father" of American poetry. He certainly has influenced many modern poets, William Carlos Williams, for instance, or Alan Ginsberg. He's influenced me, too. Whitman taught us that poems could sing without a regular rhyme scheme and without highfallootin' diction. Whitman taught us to appreciate the music in the barmaid's banter, to marvel at the fireworks exploding from a teamster's curse.

How can you call that poetry? Lots of people are still asking this question. Your poems sound like someone talking, they say. Isn't that just prose? Well, yes, a clear demarcation between poetry and prose no longer exists. Some poetry is very prosaic. Some prose is very poetic. To explore this issue, I recommend reading an exceptionally brilliant poem called "One Morning Shoeing Horses" by Henry Taylor, who won the Pulitzer Prize back in the 1970s for his book *The Flying Change.* I won't say much about this poem; I'm hoping you will read it and discover its power on your own. The poem just sounds like someone talking — if you read without pausing at the end of each line. And it rhymes.

Poet's Notes: Great Aunt Ida's Last Christmas

"The more things change, the more they stay the same." When I first heard this aphorism, I was a young person, and the idea puzzled me greatly. How can things change and still stay the same? Slowly, over the years, I've come to understand. Consider, for instance, the automobile. Before Cadillacs and Buicks, we rode horses to get from place to place, or we employed horses to pull wagons and carriages. Then arose the revolutionary and world-changing notion that we could propel our carriages with the "horsepower" of an internal combustion engine. Yes, the world changed; now, we had to feed our transport gasoline instead of hay. And, yes, we could travel a bit faster and maybe in more comfort. But our lives basically stayed the same; we still needed to get out of the house and travel for work and play; we still needed roadways and maps and signs; we still needed to move our products to market. Any of you own a Ford "Mustang"?

Change is wonderful, and change is painful, especially in times of transition, shifting from the old way to the new. In the poem "Aunt Ida's Last Christmas," the elderly woman is struggling to leap from the Stone Age of radio entertainment into the Space Age world of TV. She's still the same person — a busybody, a know-it-all, cold as stone. She's convinced she's witnessed a crime because it happened right there in front of her on the TV. Before the TV, people listened to mysteries and crime stories on the radio. Maybe radio stories seemed less real than TV stories, but I don't think so. Consider the major hullabaloo over the radio broadcast of the H. G. Wells fictional "War of the Worlds." People died because they couldn't understand that the broadcaster's account of an alien invasion was theatrical fiction, just "pretend."

Think a moment about your own life. How have you struggled with change? For me, I fell behind way back in the 1970s when my classmates started wearing digital watches. The watches I'd known previously had one little dial to move the hour and minute hands round and round to adjust the time or date. These newfangled digital watches depended upon learning cutting-edge concepts — "modes" and "functions" — which paved the road for newer computer technologies headed our way. Sounds ridiculously easy now, but those ideas were shiny and unfamiliar once-upon-a-time. I fixed the problem: I stopped wearing a watch. That joke falls flat now because hardly anyone wears a watch. Now we tell time on the phone. The point is this: Old-fashioned watches, digital watches, or phones . . . we are still interested in knowing the time. Things have changed, and things have stayed the same.

What doesn't change is the tension between generations. Why is it that each elder generation thinks the newer generation isn't worth a pocket full of salt? "What's wrong with those kids?" We've all heard people say that, and, if we're old enough, we've likely heard it from our own lips, too. "Never trust anyone over thirty," said my Boomer Generation in the 60s. "Don't criticize what you can't understand," sang Bob Dylan, railing against the establishment. "Get out of the new road if you can't lend a hand," he said. The times were a-changin'. A little bit, maybe. And so much stayed the same.

Poet's Notes: How We Survived the Cuban Missile Crisis

"Life goes on," we counsel loved ones after a tragedy, "and you must go on, too." I knew a man who lost his young daughter in a sad car wreck. He had to march on, but it was a slow and almost impossible road back to some sense of normalcy. When the Twin Towers were attacked and destroyed, so many lives were lost, so many more lives thrown off center, so many lives left wobbling in chaos and grief. I remember seeing the news coverage — video of the planes hitting the towers, concrete and glass imploding, bodies falling from the sky, shock and bewilderment on faces fleeing the devastation. A stunning tragedy, and — for those of us who survived — that day remains a marker in time. We ask, "Where were you when the Twin Towers fell?" Yet, life goes on, and we had to go on, too. Even though we've resumed our daily routine, we carry that event and those images with us ever after. It's always with us, under the surface, a subtle shift of consciousness, though we've busied ourselves with shopping lists and flossing our teeth, almost as if the horror hadn't happened.

The 1950s and 60s were scary years to be a kid. We ducked under our school desks when Civil Defense sirens sounded, our anxious little brains barraged with nightmare images of mushrooming atomic firestorms roiling skyward, Hiroshima and Nagasaki scorched to cinders, naked death camp inmates milling about like zombies. Our shell-shocked fathers had come home from war with far-off looks in their eyes, and when they cast their gazes upon us, they cut holes in our hearts. I heard the term "Iron Curtain," and in my grammar school innocence, I pictured a steel slab reaching to the clouds, impenetrable, blocking the sunlight and casting darkness across the globe. I heard the term "Cold War," and I imagined Khrushchev poised with his hand on the button, a symbol of the ever-present possibility he'd launch a nuclear Armageddon. "We will bury you!" — I heard Nikita spit those words on TV over and over. Our neighbors dug bomb shelters and studied survival strategies. But how could we hide from polio, birth defects, and TB? We imagined a bogeyman under our beds or hiding in closets, but the newscasts were filled with worse than that. When we ducked under our desks, we said our prayers.

The Cuban Missile Crisis was an important moment and also a nothing moment, lost in the crush and clutter of so many other things to worry about. The crisis came and went. In the poem, "How We Survived the Cuban Missile Crisis," I'm looking back and laughing at us. Well, laughing is not the right word. Maybe the poem is a thankful sigh of relief that sometimes bad things don't happen. Crazy, too, all these years later to glimpse our pathetic survival plan for nuclear attack, huddled as we were under the basement steps. My mother had stocked nearby shelves with rows of garden vegetables sealed in glass jars. I imagined that when the missiles came crashing, the earth would shudder, and those glass jars seemed like an obvious bad idea. My mother's mutiny also seemed less than wise. Yet, next morning, we woke up much the same as always — because life goes on and we had to stumble along with it. Yes, it was a nothing moment, but it's still part of me, even today.

Poet's Notes: The Cold War at Home

As a kid, I felt in the middle — a middle-child, in mid-America, during the mid-century. I wasn't smart or dumb, tall or short, popular or unpopular; I was in the middle. Our address wasn't exactly in town, nor was it in the country. We lived in a sort of no-man's-land of empty fields and acres of pine, farmland slowly giving way to newly-constructed modest dwellings at the edge of town where the streets and gutters and sidewalks ended.

Early on, I mastered a bad habit of getting in the middle of other people's struggles. If there was a fight on the playground, I put myself in the middle and tried to referee, which rewarded me with little more than scraped elbows and a bloodied nose. This didn't stop me; I was nothing if not in the middle of the fray. Maybe I just wanted to be noticed; I was angling to define myself in some outstanding way. I wanted to be a hero. Ghandi was a big name in our grammar school history books back then, and Jesus was famous every Sunday. Both had inserted themselves into the vortex of conflict. They'd envisioned a better world and scraped their elbows and bloodied their noses, heroically calling for all sides to behave. Ghandi and Jesus became my superheroes, way more impressive than Bat Man or Green Lantern. Tales of superhuman deeds wormed their way deep in my brain.

If my parents were quarreling, I put myself in the middle. I just wanted my parents to behave. Mom and Dad were like my classmates rolling in gravel on the playground, emotionally out of control, wrestling each other to gain a dubious upper hand. I trembled inside, but I kept a calm look on my face and wouldn't let anyone guess my anxiety. I tried to referee. In school each Friday, we read from a flimsy newsprint periodical called "The Weekly Reader." I read about the DEW Line, radar installations along our northern border, a "Distant Early Warning" system to detect incoming Russian nuclear warheads. I was in the early grades; even at that tender age I was the DEW line at home, and I knew it. I fortified my outpost to keep an eye on both sides of all quarrels. I lay awake in bed listening for trouble. I held my breath, heroically vigilant, when Mom gave Dad the cold shoulder, or when Dad sat reading the newspaper, his face hidden, his breath quickened with agitation.

I tell this all because I've encountered in my classrooms so many young adults who soldiered forward through childhoods one shade of pain or another similar to mine. They feel invisible, overlooked, and they are strangers to themselves and their own needs, having endeavored so diligently to help everyone else get along. They're in the middle — not abused exactly, nor neglected — just unrecognized in fundamental ways. You know who you are, and this little essay is for each and every one of you. Sad to say, but it took decades for me to overcome a lasting resentment toward my parents who were so involved in protecting themselves and their own hurt feelings that they forgot to protect me and had few clues I was feeling anything at all. In a cold war, that's how it goes.

Poet's Notes: Peace

When I try to imagine my father with a machine gun amidst a fire-fight, I go blank. I've never fought in a war. I can vividly conjure in my mind lots of things I've never experienced firsthand, but here I fail. "You just can't understand unless you've been there." Combat veterans have told me this in class. I'm the teacher, and they are struggling to instruct me; they're understandably frustrated when I push them to clarify trauma beyond my powers of imagination.

One young vet brought to class a poster of the "Johari Window," a tool to help us understand ourselves. He'd borrowed it from a psychologist at the Vet's Hospital. The "window" has four quadrants: 1.) What I and others know of me — my public self. 2.) What others know of me, but I don't — my blind spots. 3.) What I know of me, and others don't — my hidden self. 4.) What I don't know of me, and no one else does either — my unknown self. It's this fourth quadrant, the "unknown self," which intrigues me most because it offers some insight into how I might make sense of my father in wartime. Under extreme stress or trauma, unknown parts of us are revealed. This is what my students were trying to teach me when they said, "You can't understand unless you've been there." This is why I can't imagine my father with a machine gun blasting at the enemy.

My father fought in the Battle of the Bulge, a foot soldier shouldering a big gun, while other soldiers trailed him, lugging his ammo. Even writing that sentence, the scene seems surreal to me. Under fire, what did my father discover about himself? I knew him as a congenial, soft-spoken man, a harmonizer, a people pleaser. The war stories he told his kids were tales of lasting and essential human goodness arising amidst ugliness and suffering. He shared his meal rations with civilians begging at the gate to his platoon's fenced encampment. For this, he said, he was almost court-martialed, but he did it anyway. The rations contained chewing gum, and he'd save that treat for one particular ragged child who had befriended him. The Battle of the Bulge lasted five horrifying weeks, midwinter; 89,000 American soldiers died. What stories did my father choose not to tell, or couldn't tell?

I suspect my father discovered in combat his own "heart of darkness." I suspect this revelation saddened him ever after, and sometimes his face paled, his eyes went blank, and he'd turn away from us to keep his internal battles hidden. Our petty quarrels and discomforts must have seemed senseless to him, and of course they were, though we were blind to that because we lacked our father's hard-earned perspective. He'd glimpsed the mysteries hidden inside his soul, that fourth quadrant of the window. He knew things we couldn't know. This is as far as I can climb in imagining my father's wartime nightmares. When he said, "Give me some peace, please," he was talking about more than hoping his kids would quit bickering.

Poet's Notes: Broke

What is a "good" man? My father showed little interest in pondering philosophical questions. "A good provider," would have been his answer. A good man holds a steady job, laboring unflinchingly paycheck to paycheck, year to year. "Keep your nose to the grindstone," was his best advice. As a kid, I imagined a determined man sitting at the grinding wheel, gritting his teeth, honing his nose sharp as a blade. "Buckle down," he'd admonish me when the teacher reported I'd failed to complete an assignment. Work was his solution to almost any problem. My father was suspicious of anyone who sat in one place too long, or anyone who yawned midday. "What you need," he'd say, "is a job."

A young teen during the Great Depression, my father watched his father scramble for pennies enough to put bread on the table. His father, he said, had "lost" the farm. To my kid-brain, that sounded odd. How could you lose something that big? No, he explained, the bankers took it. President Hoover and the bankers were the bad guys; my father harbored a deep bitterness toward men in suits and ties. A "desk job" wasn't real work. My grandfather was buried before I was born, so what little I knew of him I learned from his son, my dad. After he'd been evicted from the farmstead, my grandfather became a "drayman," which means he drove a horse cart up and down the streets, calling out for rags and scrap metal. He kept his nose to the grindstone.

My mother's job was "housewife." She stayed home and cooked and cleaned and trudged up and down the basement stairs with relentless loads of laundry. Most of my friends' mothers also stayed home and relied on hubby's paycheck. "A woman's work is never done," my mother sometimes complained. This meant she had to get up early to fry eggs and bacon for the hungry mouths at the breakfast table. She'd pack a lunch for her husband. She'd button us into our coats and wave as we walked toward school. Then she did chores; she ironed everything, even bed sheets and pillow cases; she sewed her own clothes and our sister's clothes; she "darned" socks, which meant she repaired holes by weaving and stitching them closed with heavy thread, a lost art. By the time we arrived home again from school, she was busy concocting a casserole for supper. Then she did the dishes. Then she swept the floors. You can't say she didn't have a "job." She kept her nose to the grindstone. My father didn't want it any other way, not because he desired to keep her from venturing into the world at large, but because it was the mark of a "good" man, a good provider, if his wife stayed home.

When the mill teetered, jobs were eliminated and workers were "laid off." For a man like my father, unemployment was an unbearable black mark on his soul. He measured his worthiness as a man by the paychecks he provided. It must have shamed him to stand in line for "public relief," which is what we now call "welfare." But he was broke, he said. I could see the agony of helplessness in his eyes. Yes, he was broken.

Poet's Notes: The Test

When my siblings and I gather to reminisce about our shared family life, we discover we've been raised in separate worlds. Specifics I remember of a particular happening are often at odds with what my siblings recall of the same event. Sometimes entire episodes are the subject of dispute. Did they happen, or not? Is there no common reality? In the poem "The Test," I'm recounting a childhood memory I've held vividly in mind since early youth, an occurrence I'd swear is fact, albeit somewhat surreal. My brothers disagree; according to them, Dad's asking us to drop our drawers to check our privates for radioactive contamination is a fiction I've contrived in my own hyperactive imagination. Is it possible we can tell ourselves a story so often we convince ourselves it's true?

"Confabulation" is a word psychologists use to describe how we remember generalities of a particular experience, and we invent the specifics to fill in the gaps of what we haven't exactly recorded. We construct or "confabulate" the details because it's scary to accept the notion that a hefty chunk of our personal histories exists only in the stories we tell ourselves and that the accuracy of our memories is deeply flawed. "Humankind," said T. S. Eliot, "cannot bear very much reality."

Facts are important. But how important are they? Einstein said, "Not everything that counts can be counted." Okay, I just researched that "quote" online and discovered that experts dispute the origin of these noteworthy words. More important than the attribution of this quote is the idea it contains. The idea is this: Many important truths can't be expressed by quantifying data or cataloging facts. I'd add to Einstein's quote by saying that the validity of our memories can't be measured by how accurately they accord with someone else's version of the same reminiscence. The truth of a matter may lie somewhere outside or beyond the facts.

As a poet, I'm interested in telling what facts alone might not reveal. So I alter the facts to get at deeper truths — the common conundrums of our shared "human condition." Well . . . that won't hold up in the courtroom, won't do on a police report, won't excuse sloppy journalism, won't forgive errors in a history textbook. Why shouldn't a poem be held to the same standards? The answer to this, I think, can be found in Samuel Taylor Coleridge's advice that we approach a poem with a "willing suspension of disbelief," which (in part) is the act of putting aside our stubborn need for accurate fact.

A student of mine once wrote a poem about a terrible wreck in which there were three people snugged side-by-side in the pickup — the writer, her boyfriend, and her sister. The writer and her boyfriend were injured and hospitalized. The sister escaped unscathed. The point of the poem was to show how the writer and her boyfriend deepened their relationship as their bones mended. *Throw the sister out of the poem before the crash,* I advised. The sister only gets in the way of the story; she unnecessarily diverts the reader's attention from the author's main message. Inexperienced writers may harbor a misplaced fidelity to facts; it was an uphill challenge for me to convince this young woman she was free, for the poem's sake, to exclude her sister.

I envy how my grandchildren enjoy pretending. As a kid, I treasured glorious afternoons exploring imaginary landscapes, sailing the high seas, hacking my way through jungles, riding my horse across the rolling plains. As an adult — as a poet — I'm resolute in keeping my imagination well-oiled and ready to roll. I'll steer around the facts as needed to arrive at where I want to go. Besides, sometimes it's just plain fun to make stuff up.

Poet's Notes: Things Got Worse

Relationships shift and change color gradually over time, a nuanced progression from one day into the next, almost unnoticeable. Sometimes there's the one big event a person can point to and say, "That's the day I fell in love," or "That's the day I knew I'd leave him." What interests me is when there's not a big event; everything seems normal, yet, over time, relationships drift into unfamiliar landscapes where the person we thought we understood so well now seems hardly recognizable. It's like sleeping on a train: So much goes past while your eyes are shut, preoccupied with your dreams. You step down to the loading platform in a strange town, wondering how you've arrived where you are.

Growing up is like that, too. Sometimes big events become the mileposts of our narrative, but most of the time not. We outgrow our shoes, one size at a time, hardly aware that the old feet are gone and new feet have replaced them. A mother marks a child's height with a penciled notch on the door frame. "How did she grow so tall?" — can't hear it happen, can't see it happen. Seems like one day you're bending down to hug your kid, and the next morning she's towering above you, and the roles are reversed.

Writing students say, "I've nothing to write about. My life is so normal, so boring." To me, these young writers are missing the point entirely. Long ago I read a book by a writing teacher who talked about "fabulous realities." Reality, he said, is more fabulous than fiction. He challenged his students to view the mundane with fresh eyes in order to glimpse the extraordinary nature of all things ordinary. Our day-to-day "same old, same old" is rich with fascinating strangeness.

Try this experiment: Close your eyes. Just sit and breathe. Now let your lids snap open. Imagine you have been transported here from outer space. In this frame of mind, the familiar turns unfamiliar, foreign and exotic. Even small objects and events seem to glow suddenly, marvelous and puzzling. When I first moved to Montana from Iowa, I felt like I'd landed on a far-off planet. "Nothing ever happens here. My life is boring," my students told me. Our classrooms were a short drive from the jaw-dropping splendor of Glacier National Park. Grizzly bears mauled hikers, and mountain lions stalked unsuspecting joggers. Forest fires raged across the late-summer-night horizon, and in winter, the twilight blazed with Northern Lights. As a writing teacher, I coax students to recognize and write about fabulous realities. "Now the eyes of my eyes are opened," wrote e. e. cummings, and he's a great example of someone who could appreciate what so many of us overlook. Our world is colorless and boring only because we are blind.

In the poem "Things Got Worse," I'm pinpointing a moment in my tween years when my father's godlike image began to tarnish. "Not much of a tree," I say to him. This is not a big event, but it's one of several accumulated instances in which I began to see my father differently. After I said what I said, I saw my father's weakness and shame. I'd hurt him, and until then, I hadn't known that was possible.

Poet's Notes: Wesley's Playland

Which of us hasn't felt an inner primitive urge to walk on the "wild side"? We are taught to be "good" children. My parents, my church, my school expected me to be upstanding, to follow the rules. My parents, my pastor, my teachers assumed I would accept the standards of my community unquestioningly, and yet I began to question. On the outside, I was well-behaved, and I was rewarded with pats on the back. My elders beheld me and beamed their satisfied smiles. On the inside, I felt like I was faking it. Something adventurous, rebellious, and playful in me wanted to express itself, but I was afraid to explore these callings. I had an angel on one shoulder and a devil on the other. I was expected to listen only to the angel, and the angel would triumph over my less-than-angelic desires.

Readers are curious to know if Wesley was a "real" person. There's an irony in that question. Wesley was real in that he was genuine. He was misguided, maybe, but he was true to himself, uninhibited, unconstrained by anyone else's narrow expectations. The angel on his one shoulder and the devil on his other shoulder weren't in constant debate and warfare. His angel and his devil were pals. He seemed vibrant and alive, more so than most of us, because he wasn't faking it. His soul had long ago rejected labels of good and bad; he didn't have to decide one or the other. He could be both. He could be whole, and I envied him for that. I knew several Wesley-like characters in my youth, and one of them was inside of me, that face in the mirror who maybe still hid from others but no longer could hide from himself.

I remember my mother once catching me in the act of petty crime. She'd baked some treats, and I'd eaten more than my share. I knew, even as a small child, that I was selfish and greedy; the sweets I'd purloined were deliciously irresistible. As I chewed and swallowed, I shuddered with a devilish joy — until my mother's scolding cut my moment of victory short. Worse than her words of admonishment, the look of deep disappointment on her face let me know I'd punctured a hole in her inflated image of me as a good boy. By this limited perspective, I should not only be the kind of boy who'd never enjoy the satisfaction of forbidden pleasure, but the kind of boy who'd never desire forbidden pleasures in the first place. Recently, I saw a movie in which a fourth-grade boy is enthusiastically searching the dictionary for "dirty" words, some of which were simply the common names of our God-given genitalia. A classmate seated nearby recognizes what the boy is up to. "Oh, you're bad," she says. But she says it with an undercover smile, meaning his lust is part of the whole of what it is to be human, meaning she's felt the same, too. The girl's response is humane. She doesn't view the boy's character to be anything more or less than the rest of us.

The Roman playwright, Terence, wrote: "I am a human being. Nothing human is alien to me." I wish I could have said these words to my mother when I was seven years old and my lips and chin were dusted with powdered-sugar evidence of my plunder.

Poet's Notes: Weasel Shit

I recently filled out a reference questionnaire for a student applying for employment. The questionnaire asked me to rank the student's abilities in all the usual categories — punctuality, reliability, honesty, etc. One question surprised me: "Is the applicant able to laugh at him/herself?"

Humor is one of those characteristics which define our "humanness," though I've seen ravens play tricks and laugh, and I suspect my dog gets a kick out of watching me bumble. So maybe we aren't the only species with a funny-bone, but I've never seen ravens or dogs or any other animals laugh at themselves. Also, look around, there's a lot of our own kind who can't seem to see the humor in their special brand of stupidity. I've been at the conference table during the dreaded "performance evaluation," and while it's refreshing to the boss when a subordinate accepts criticism graciously, when the subordinate can laugh at himself, I relish rare moments when a boss can break into a grin and laugh at herself, too. Hell, we are all hilarious on some level, aren't we?

Think for a moment about self-deprecating humor. It feels false to make a joke about a hard-earned success, and the joke falls flat. Swallow your toothbrush one morning, and you've got fodder for real comedy. It's truly self-deprecating to admit swallowing your toothbrush and hilarious to hear the story of how you survived it in the end. No pun intended. I survived a hemorrhoidectomy, and boy did everyone I told about it find it funny. I couldn't find cause to giggle until the pain subsided. I gritted my teeth to be the butt of everyone else's jokes till, finally, I could laugh and make my butt the butt of my own jokes, too. People don't make wisecracks about kidney transplants. Why is a butt so funny?

Get up at a poetry reading where people are bored and half in dread of what comes next and announce the title of your poem "Weasel Shit," and suddenly everyone's awake and ready to howl. Poetry can be painfully "highbrow." It is quick refreshment to hear a poem about the poet's struggles with the same stupidity each of us battles in ourselves every day. The funniest part of the poem is the two kids mishearing "weeds and shit" as "weasel shit." But a good story squeezes a central theme to yield more juice than you thought possible in the first place. It's humorous to consider how the two boys fear the old farmer, when really he turns out to be a kindly old man with a talent for mumbling. Then picture two boys poking sticks at turds all day and cataloging poop . . . well, who wouldn't smile?

A Mesquakie Indian friend once told me that if someone farted at a tribal council meeting, all serious business would happily be put on hold as joking and teasing and laughter ensued. I can't imagine the same response to flatulence in our state legislature, though a lot of hot air smells funny each term. Isn't it more humane to laugh at our "humanness" than it is to hide it? Why be shamed by our biology? If we all laughed at ourselves, we'd be laughing together, wouldn't we?

Poet's Notes: Lewis and Clark the Hard Way

What captures your imagination? That word, "capture" . . . isn't that exactly how it goes? We are "struck" by inspiration, the best and most powerful of which seems like arrows launched in space and landing dead-center inside one lucky unsuspecting soul or another. How fortunate we are when that lucky soul is our own! Some of us are marked as more likely targets than most, more open to influence than not, an aspect of our character which leads us into adventures, some glorious and transforming, some fraught with pain.

I was never a "good" student, but I've always been curious. My best teachers recognized my thirst for learning and forgave me for my lack of achievement, for lost homework, for sitting in a corner distracted by squirrels arguing in the trees outside the classroom window. They honored my propensity to wander, to follow inspiration down its own twisted path. "I have never let my schooling get in the way of my education," said Mark Twain.

The saga of Lewis and Clark captured my grade-school imagination. Here were two pals who set out into the wild to discover what was there. These weren't soldiers out to subdue and conquer enemy forces. These weren't pirates out to plunder and brawl. These weren't fortune hunters searching for gold. Instead, Lewis and Clark were all about learning. To me, as a kid, the Corps of Discovery seemed a sort of dream-school in which you paddled into the unknown just for the sheer joy of knowing more. Imagine that: No test scores. No grades. No one scolding you to sit up and pay attention. Best of all . . . no one sending you to the principal's office for losing the trail and ambling off in the wrong direction.

As in the poem "Lewis and Clark the Hard Way," I've aspired often in my life to adventure blindly forward, guided by inspiration and an undying desire to learn. I've discovered I'm a romantic, an irrepressible optimist . . . and I chronically jump into action, underestimating the stress and difficulty of situations from which more realistic souls might step aside, adjudging the enterprise too risky, too steep to climb, too much paddling upstream. Can you understand how these markers in my character — romanticism and optimism — have blessed me and cursed me also? I hear an adventure story like Lewis and Clark, and I picture nothing but blue skies, wholesome campfire cooking, and friendly natives waving sorrowfully when in the morning we must leave their village and paddle onward. It's not in my nature to think of danger, quarrelsome comrades, sickness, bugs, and near-starvation. So, more often than not, I'm a bit dumbfounded when the real world collides with my rose-colored expectations. In this way, I'm cursed.

On the other hand, if I were a more realistic and practical personality, I'd likely never venture beyond my driveway. With less than the normal quota of dread, I march into this day and the next, rose-colored glasses intact. Yes, I discover hardships unforeseen, and often I fail to achieve my naïve and unrealistic destinations. Yet I keep on keeping on. In this short lifetime, I want to know and experience all there is of this fascinating complex planet and beyond. I'm not inclined to allow troubles I haven't dreamt of yet to restrain me, captured as I am by inspiration. In this way, I'm blessed.

Poet's Notes: Murder

I was born and raised in a no-name town in the middle of nowhere. That's how I felt, as if our sleepy burg was an island surrounded by vast open oceans. Outsiders seldom walked our streets — unless they were washed ashore by accident — and they stayed for only as long as it took to build an escape vessel and set sail for brighter lands anywhere beyond our nowhere. Elsewhere, tycoons in glistening skyscrapers negotiated arms deals with foreign powers . . . while my parents argued over the grocery list. Elsewhere, genius and ambition in white coats launched John Glenn into orbit . . . while our city fathers' idea of breathtaking progress meant a stoplight at the corner of First and Main.

We left our doors unlocked and walked the streets alone after dark, unafraid. *Nothing happens here,* we thought. *Crime happens elsewhere, never here.* We assumed the future would bring only more of the same. We were asleep and didn't know it; we hadn't heard the wake-up call . . . yet. Then one unsuspecting sunrise, a local girl was found dead near the railroad trestle which spanned the river dividing our town. She'd been stabbed. She'd been beaten. The number of stab wounds and the severity of her bludgeoning increased to monstrous dimensions as gossip spread neighbor to neighbor.

We were shocked, trembling and dumbfounded. Yet . . . sorry if this sounds cold . . . even as a kid I detected that most of us, including myself, were somewhat glad to gain notice, to hear our town named on the evening news, to spy honest-to-God detectives from the FBI scouring for clues in the cinders along our humble rail yards. Then, too, I heard teachers and storekeepers assuring one another that the killer surely wasn't one of us, and I wondered at that. No resident of this place could possibly knife a young waitress? Why did we find that so impossible to comprehend? Hairdressers concurred with the butcher who confided in the mailman, and we all concluded the culprit was an ex-boyfriend from elsewhere, or the bad guy was a gangland thug from *Dragnet* dramas on late-night TV. I began to see our town was small, and we were small, too, smaller than I'd imagined, childlike and naïve.

So the wake-up call came, and I, for one, continued a degree more wide-eyed ever after. Isn't this exactly how we mature, one wake-up alarm after another, some whispering us from our slumbers, some screaming us awake? Small town life can be a cocoon, an insulated bubble, and some people prefer to domicile where headlines are seldom made, where one day succeeds the next without rippling the prevailing calm.

Still, no abode, no matter how simple and tranquil, can shield us from the greater world (and darker realities) inevitably knocking at our door. In hindsight, I'm bemused by my youthful simpleminded innocence. *Nothing will happen here,* I thought. Little did I know one day the fabric of this illusion would unravel so completely. Murder in my hometown caused a seismic shift in my brain. I moved out of a state of Innocence and into a state of Knowledge, out of the Eden of blissful ignorance, into the wilderness of uncertainty. My illusions were dispelled, and I'm grateful for knowing now — no matter how unsettling — what I didn't know then.

Poet's Notes: Goodbye, Wesley

I hesitate to confess: Wesley is a character I've constructed. In saying this, I hope not to have spoiled the poem, to have broken the reader's trust. Wesley is a patchwork of several pals from my youth, boys I admired for all I was not. Wesley is unreserved and worldly. I was shy and naïve. Wesley is a realist, a person of action. I was a dreamer and a consummate idealist from the day I was born. Writers make a lot of things up, and they also borrow heavily from their own experience, their families, their neighborhoods, their friends. The result is often neither fact nor fiction but somewhere between. The goal is to make it seem real, to convince the reader that the story is told exactly as it happened. So don't assume, dear reader, that my poems are autobiographical, even though they may seem so. Then again, I should be pleased to have subdued the reader's sense of what's real and what's not. It's complicated, this twisted relationship, you and me and words on the page.

Another confession: I was in love with Wesley . . . not all the Wesleys, just one in particular. In saying this, I can imagine raised eyebrows, and I'm heavy-hearted when I see best friends anywhere, two boys (or two girls) communing intimately, each having partnered with the other in matters of deepest concern. Isn't that love? Why do we resist using that word for same-sex pals? I'm heavy-hearted because I know so few people will understand.

Gary, the boy in question, was in fifth grade, and I was in the grade above. Each morning he'd move from his grade to mine for math class because he was smarter than his own grade. He'd sit quietly and let us all try to puzzle out an answer to the computation problem on the chalkboard, and when we were all stumped, the teacher would nod permission for Gary to share with us the answer he'd figured easily in his head. Others in my class resented this interloper for making us look slow, but I was smitten. I'd never seen such genius, such confident calm.

Gary lived alone with his mother, a "dee-vor-cee" as our parents called her. She was a new teacher at the high school, and this was way different from our mothers, who called themselves "homemakers" and wore aprons and studied cookbooks. I think I was in love with Gary's mother, too. When Gary and I showed up after school, she'd sit with us and talk, really talk . . . and she'd listen to what I had to say like no adult I'd known till then. I felt honored and accepted. Sadly, my family made mean-spirited jokes about how much time Gary and I spent together.

Gary and I mostly played basketball. He was taller than I was, an enthusiastic athlete, and I was short for my age and couldn't dribble more than a few steps without the ball escaping my untalented hands. Gary tutored me, and I did my best to learn what I could about the game. "Do you suddenly love basketball, or do you love him?" my brothers taunted me. They were right. I was defenseless. I felt wrong.

Now this: Did I just weave a small fiction in the last few paragraphs? How will you ever be sure? And does it matter?

Poet's Notes: Let's Hope This Thing Blows Over Soon

Once-upon-a-time, there was a brutal war in Vietnam, a small country in Southeast Asia. My junior-high classmates and I could scarcely locate Vietnam on the globe, and we had no idea what this bloody conflict was all about. Our heads were filled with fog, but this war would wake us, year by year, as we neared the threshold of conscription, leaving us to worry through long, dark nights of sleeplessness. I say "once-upon-a-time" because the tangled, sad history of this nightmare now seems like a fairy tale, scary and surreal. Five decades later, with my fingers on the keyboard pecking out these words — The War in Vietnam — I'm yet filled with dread, and the ghost of those painful years scrapes its rusty chains across my gut.

I've memorized Wilfred Owen's "Dulce et Decorum Est," a painfully frightening poem, a horrifying glimpse into the inhumane consequence of political madness. Owen's war was World War I, dubbed the "war to end all wars," an optimistic assessment soon to be dispelled. My father's war was World War II, the Battle of the Bulge. When his kids requested bedtime tales of combat heroism, he'd look away and shake his head incredulously, his nightmare still lingering, scary and surreal. That war ended with a bang — Hiroshima and Nagasaki — and surely now we could all live in lasting peace and civility. But the Korean War exploded soon after; my father and his buddies from the mill sat on stools in the Vet's Club Bar, toasting round after round in silent acceptance of never-ending bloodshed. *Dulce et decorum est pro patria mori* — how sweet and noble to die for one's homeland — my father and his buddies would have offered a sorry nod to the haunting irony of those words.

Next was Vietnam, my turn, and I refused to go. It's a long story I won't recount here, but imagine being fourteen years old and watching your father's troubled face at the supper table while, on the TV nearby, Walter Cronkite recited the day's "body count." Vietnam was the first war we could watch live from a distance via the magic of electronic broadcasting. I saw a Vietnamese officer (the regime we supported) lift his pistol to a young man's head and blow his skull open. I saw a Buddhist monk douse his shaven cranium and long robes with gasoline . . . and set himself ablaze on a busy Saigon street corner. How was I to make sense of these images? When the recruiters came to our school, I didn't believe a single sweet and noble word they had to say.

Times have changed, and times haven't changed at all. I mention The War in Vietnam to young adults in my classes today, and their eyes glaze over as if I'm talking about ancient history, the stuff they were coerced to memorize in high school and tossed aside as soon as the semester was ended. American young men and women in uniform invaded Iraq, and I thought, *Let's hope this thing blows over soon.* We inserted our troops in Afghanistan, and I thought, *Let's hope this thing blows over soon.* The body count in Afghanistan has been mounting now for 18 years. Will it ever end? Will the madness ever end?

Poet's Notes: Hitchhiker

Somewhere along the way, or maybe straight out of the womb, I've been anointed with magic pixie dust. Some days I'm amazed to look back at my earlier life, and I've no clear explanation of how or why I'm still here. I once awoke in the sage desert of eastern Oregon, having blindly thrown my sleeping bag on the ground only a few short steps from the edge of The Crooked River Gorge, an awesome crevasse in the earth. I'd stumbled my way from the highway in darkness and slept three paces short of an early exit to the ever-after, miraculously oblivious to dangers near at hand. Yet, when I opened my eyes that morning, I was flooded with awe and joy.

Near Oslo, Norway, I once looked a Mack truck in the headlights headed smack toward my young innocent face in the passenger seat of a Volvo stopped in the wrong lane at a railroad crossing. I could see the truck driver's panic as he braked and downshifted. I sat unmovable as stone, though not because I'm brave. I just knew I'd walk away unscathed. That sounds foolish, even as I write this. I apologize to the gods for that. I've been lucky. I've been blessed. I've been dusted with magic.

The poem "Hitchhiker" is a pivotal moment in the verse-play, *Someday I'd Write This Down.* What shift, what transformation takes place? Let me say this: Much like we grow out of one pair of shoes into the next, we outgrow our childhood consciousness into levels increasingly more expansive and mature. During the long night depicted in the poem, "Working on My Words," the Boy suddenly becomes conscious that he is, like his father and his father's mother, "one of them," a living being, sprung from a long line of those who'd walked on this earth before us. In "Hitchhiker," the Boy becomes the Young Man. He's moved into a new consciousness, much like the caterpillar sheds his cocoon. (An apt symbol — the Boy discarding his sleeping bag like a caterpillar sheds his cocoon. It just happened that way, literally and figuratively. I didn't plant that symbol intentionally. I'm surprised to find it here, amazed once again how language, how the earth at our feet, how our innocent actions . . . are all continually revealing who we are and what it means to be alive, how the real world and the imagined world surely seem constructed by some hand larger than our own.)

Literature is full of "coming of age" stories. Folktales offer abundant accounts of the "hero's journey" in which the young man or woman leaves home and transforms internally after facing external challenges. All of us, of course, have completed journeys of our own, though so many of us are unaware. Poets, on the other hand, live mythically, composing the story to tell — the saga of our lives. We tell the tale as it unfolds, even though the ending remains a mystery to ourselves. Sure, we bend the facts, embellish the highs and lows, shape the plot to suit the audience, or to please our whimsy. I was born to do this work; I'm the Scribe — not the Captain, or Soldier, or Scholar, or Healer, or Priest. I'm the guy who writes it down.

When I began scribbling in my notebook the first draft of the poem "Hitchhiker," I had no idea I'd write . . . "waking / amidst pungent sage, letting the sun's new rays / seep in; absolutely certain I'd carry with me / the joy of this and someday write it down." The poem reminded me I'd plummeted to earth in a ball of flame, as had so many Scribes before. Had I landed where I stood shivering that morning by accident? Or by design? I woke alone, lost, and half frozen in the early glare of the daystar and the menacing splendor of The Crooked River Gorge, my shoes dancing in the dust, my soul singing praise to the sky.

Poet's Notes: Let's Get Stupid

If you can't beat 'em, join 'em. Do you hear, in those words, a note of sad resignation, of hopelessness? During the War in Vietnam, I lived in the "land of the free," but I felt like a pawn manipulated by powerful men who wouldn't think twice about marching me into combat as little more than cannon fodder. I'll never forget this scene: My older brother is decked out in a bandana headband, long beard and shoulder-length hair, Mexican serape, tattered jeans, and sandals. He's on the sidewalk, rounding a corner by the bank on Main, and he collides with a local businessman of means and influence. "Why don't you take a bath and get a haircut?" the man hisses. My brother replies calmly with the cool arrogance of a soul ready to throw himself off a bridge: "The way I see it," he says, "some people are rotten from inside out; I'm starting on the outside and working my way in." Hippies of the 60s preached the goodness of smoking dope and popping hallucinogens for the sake of consciousness transformation (à la Timothy Leary), but wasn't getting high — in hindsight — just a desperate escape? I heard in my brother's words a sad note of resignation, of hopelessness. My translation: I'd sooner destroy myself than die in your war.

Upon my eighteenth birthday, I walked into the local Selective Service Office (even small towns like my own had one) to register for the military draft. Failing to register was a felony, punishable with imprisonment. I didn't want to go to war. I didn't want to go to jail. I just wanted the whole damn mess to leave me alone, but that wasn't going to happen. Some of my classmates enlisted, some allowed themselves to be drafted without a fuss. I resisted. Was I right? Was I wrong? This was the first real moral dilemma I'd grappled with, and it wrestled me to the ground, dragged me through the mud.

After high school, I volunteered for the graveyard shift on our local Teen Crisis Line. Night after night, I pressed the phone receiver to my ear and listened to a litany of sad resignation and hopelessness, kids on acid trips scared out of their wits, some who'd fried their brains beyond ever coming back. We called them drug "burn-outs." "He's a burn-out," we'd say, meaning he spoke in half sentences and spent hours standing on the curb staring at dog shit in the gutter. That sounds mean and angry, I know, but these were kids I'd played kickball with at recess, neighborhood pals now turned zombie. The war had killed them before they ever got there.

"Let's get stupid," we'd say, meaning let's hope we can get high enough to distract us from dread. There's a silly side of this, and I hope my poem brings that forward also. We were stupid like sloppy drunks are stupid, hilarious and slapstick. We were Moe, Larry, and Curly; we could hit ourselves and each other over the head with a two-by-four and barely feel it. Fact is, it seemed like fun, something to brag about in the morning. Ha-ha, I nearly died. It's possible to cover over pain with more pain.

Poet's Notes: Action

     A psychology professor once told me that there are two kinds of dreamers: One kind sits home and dreams but takes no action. The other kind takes steps each day, baby steps, to nudge his dreams into reality. "I'm moving to Venice Beach," one of my hometown buddies might announce loudly, "in nine days." Nine days later, he's standing on the same street corner as nine days before. Nine months later, nothing has changed, but he's amplified his vow to accomplish his big move. Nine years later . . . well, you get the point. People get stuck. All our big talk means nothing if we can't buttress our aims with actions.

     I'm uneasy about deadlines; I procrastinate until the eleventh hour to make good on an obligation. In general, I rally for a breathtaking final dive at the finish line. Some of us need a deadline, or we sit and yack about our plan to prove the Earth is round, but we never gather our ships and crews and set sail . . . until we hear the panic siren seconds before the gates of opportunity slam shut. What happens when there are no deadlines? What will spur us to act upon our ambitions, to get off the couch, buy the plane ticket, write the first chapter, shop for the ring? "Between the idea / And the reality / Between the motion / And the act," wrote T. S. Eliot, "Falls the Shadow." Think of solitary Abraham Lincoln educating himself in his log cabin. Think of Walt Whitman penning poem after poem despite lifelong ridicule and obscurity. Think of Frederick Douglass, a slave with an unquenchable hunger for learning, for truth, for justice. Or think of any number of inventors, investors, and innovators who march to the drumbeat of internal motivations . . . while the Hollow Man fails to inch forward without a hot poker threatening the seat of his pants.

     Then, too, I recently heard about research (www.youarenotsosmart.com) which shows that the more we boldly announce our plans, the less likely we will achieve them. When we ingratiate ourselves with admiration and praise for deeds yet undone, we drain the vitality of our aspiration. This speaks volumes as to why my hometown buddy never bought his bus ticket to Venice Beach. Also, this explains why writers squirm when asked, "What's the plot of your novel-in-progress?" The "spirit which moves us" dies when it's pinned and displayed on the mounting board before it's morphed into an angel with its own wings.

     I was a freshman at the University of Wisconsin during the turbulent anti-war chaos of 1969-70. We were passionate and loud in our convictions, though many of us felt helpless to act. We threw stones on State Street, smashing windows of our favorite hangouts. What had we accomplished? Someone stole an airplane and boldly dropped bombs on a munitions depot just outside of town. The bombs were duds, the plane abandoned in a farmer's cornfield. One big bomb did explode one fateful night at the Army Math Research Center, killing a physics prof. What good did that do? *Between the motion and the act, falls the shadow.* Someone threw a metal folding chair across hot wires at a power substation near our dorm, and the neighborhood went dark. We sat in candle light, smoking dope and talking tough, our textbooks abandoned, our dreams and our futures wafting out the open window, lost in the black.

Poet's Notes: Kissing

Well, you see, I was the only one with a car, my father's car, a big old station wagon. This made me suddenly attractive to a certain type of girl. We were thrown together at a YMCA camp deep in the woods, a couple dozen high schoolers who'd been recruited for a weekend retreat, a "consciousness raising" event, led by a pastor from one of those new hip churches where people played guitars and sang folk songs. We huddled around a big fireplace in the lodge, sitting cross-legged on the floor. We talked about religion. We talked about politics. We all agreed the Vietnam War must end, but before we could find peace in the world we'd pray for peace in our hearts. All afternoon, we basked in lots of happy, contrived concordance like that. Then a big spaghetti feed, and soon after . . . our hormones needed attention. We were itching to put aside the humorless demands of consciousness-raising in favor of more primitive urges. Outside, a powdery snow was mounding, but the moon shone through the clouds with a mystical, magical luminescence, calling to our groins. When the pastor and our chaperones readied for bed, we smiled like good boys and girls and promised we'd crawl into our sleeping bags soon, all of us knowing this was a bald-faced lie.

You can imagine what mischief we accomplished that night, unbuttoning as best we could, as if by slipping out of shirts and jeans we were shedding our childhoods, giggling and groaning toward opening adult wings. I'll spare you the details. We say, "Love makes fools of us all." There's a note of pain, a note of humor, a note of truth in those words. Who among us hasn't fumbled through darkness in pursuit of love, entranced by hormonal imperatives surging in his veins?

As an older man, one thing I know for sure: The "art of love" is indeed an art and requires decades of complicated and determined practice. That's both good news and bad. When I find myself harkening back to my own first encounters with Cupid's slings and arrows, I'm most often lying wide-eyed and confounded, having just awakened from a bewitching dream. The dream itself I might not remember, but I'm tasting an emotional residue left in its passing. Wave upon wave, images from earlier days come flooding over me, and on a good night I laugh a little incredulous sigh to examine again the ridiculous, feverish, groping, desperate animal I am. On a not-so-good night, I cringe with shame, regret, and humiliation. I've been wounded in love, and I've injured some innocent others along the way. "I've looked at love from both sides now," sang Judy Collins in the turbulence of the 1960s.

My poem, "Kissing," is meant to be humorous, mostly. The weekend retreat was a success; my consciousness was indeed raised, or changed at least, though not in the manner our pastor had intended. The most enduring lessons usually happen to us outside the classroom, no? I'm pretty sure the pastor and chaperones knew we'd snuck away, but no one said anything the next day. Our little escapade had filled us with questions. We talked on and on about God and war; the prescribed curriculum ignored more personal and urgent matters at hand. As a teacher, I keep this incident in mind. Sometimes, while I'm standing in the classroom flapping my arms and singing my lessons as best I'm able, I know in my heart I'm not getting my message across. I teach what I know, what I think is of value, but I can surmise by the faraway look in a student's eyes . . . .

Poet's Notes: You Don't Sound So Good

So much we take for granted. We all know this, but we don't do much about it. I hear regret in so many of my students' essays and poems, remorse for not having thanked a loved one, for having intended to communicate gratefulness but never quite getting the task accomplished. Our actions speak louder than our good intentions, and too often we lose a loved one and survive day by day afterwards with a sorry sense we've neglected an important obligation to convey what we've longed to say. I, too, have failed to let my loved ones know what's in my heart. How about you?

When my father lay dying, I lived a long ways off. My sister, who attended his bedside during his final few breaths, phoned me to say I'd better offer my last words to him, or I'd never get the chance. He couldn't speak, and my sister didn't know if he was conscious enough to comprehend, but she wisely insisted I should talk. I was caught completely off guard, speeding down a busy highway with a head full of my own worries and ambitions, most of which seemed petty all of a sudden, most of which drifted beyond me into the clouds like lost balloons.

Dad, I said, *do you remember my Milwaukee Journal paper route? Do you remember when winter came and I couldn't pedal the route, and you drove me night after night through sleet and snow?* Then I choked up and couldn't say more. I'm not the sort of person who is overcome with emotion easily, so the moment left me stunned. If I said more, I can't remember, but certainly the few words I'd offered weren't enough, unless it's true that the dead and dying know and understand a whole lot more than we do.

What I wanted to say was this: That was the most impractical, least profitable paper route imaginable. The route stretched eight miles for 21 customers, and I earned a grand fortune of $2.85 per week. Surely my dad understood the folly. Minimum wage back then was just above one dollar per hour, but I'd spend three hours a night pedaling that route, and when he graciously chauffeured me, it took at least an hour and a half and who knows how much gas. So the math alone says something about my dad's character: He'd keep quiet about what he knew were lousy wages to let his son explore the world of work on his own.

More than that, I wanted to tell him a memory I'd cherished and didn't even know I'd carried with me. One particularly wintery night along the route, I'd left a neatly-folded paper inside a customer's screen door and walked back toward my dad waiting in the car, his headlights accentuating the downpour of wet snow, the exhaust rising crimson in the taillight's steady glare. I was wet and cold; inside the car, when I shut the door, it was warm, and the radio played my father's favorite polka station. I looked at the man who sat behind the wheel, and I saw he wasn't young anymore; he was exhausted after finishing another full shift at the mill. I saw creases on his face. I saw his eyelids drooping and weary. I smelled the sawdust and sweat on his flannel shirt and shabby work pants. I listened to him humming his polka tunes. I felt loved and cared for. We drove on in silence.

Poet's Notes: Change Finds My Hometown

The War in Vietnam and the Civil Rights Movement . . . these struggles dominated the headlines in 1969. We were high-school seniors, burning hot with youthful idealism, our heads abuzz with dreams of ridding the world of war and racial injustice. We staged peace vigils in a local park. We lit candles, held hands, sang songs. We draped a banner from tree to tree: NO MORE WAR. Cars passing honked and gave us a thumbs-up, or honked and gave us the finger. Opinions were divided — this was obvious — but mostly in our little town we waved hello to neighbors and talked about the weather and the price of cheese. Vietnam seemed distant as the moon, and we heard stories on the evening news about civil rights marches and boycotts in bigger places most of us had never been and could barely imagine. Our town was peaceful. Our town was all white.

A small group of friends banded together to do what we could in support of interracial harmony. We named our group The Committee for Interracial Education. I'm not sure who we thought we might educate, but in the end, we'd mostly educated ourselves. Our eyes were opened. We learned we were ignorant and naïve — not such a bad outcome, really. Learning humility can be humiliating, and it can also be the gateway to wisdom.

We imported some young black guys from a Job Corps Center, bussed them to our town for the weekend. We pictured they'd be grateful for this opportunity to rub elbows with some sympathetic Caucasian crusaders; we'd sit with them and "rap" about fixing racial tensions, and then we'd be pals. Our local newspaper ran a little story about our plans, and suddenly we were infamous. My father came home and told me that the guys at work were calling us troublemakers. *I've got nothing against Negroes*, he said, *but why you gotta bring them up here anyways?* Over the next week, we heard that sentiment repeatedly: I'm not a racist, but . . . we're just a simmering kettle of happy little potatoes, and we don't need anyone stirring up the pot.

We learned bigger lessons when the bus arrived. These didn't seem like boys; they seemed like men, taller than we were, menacing, wary, reluctant to shake hands, and . . . well, blacker than we'd prepared for. Sitting in a meeting room at the YMCA and "rapping" lasted all of twenty minutes, with our guests looking stony-faced while us white boys did all the talking. We worked it out, sort of, and mostly spent the weekend playing basketball, though I sensed our guests were just as baffled by us as we were puzzled by them. After the bus sped off into the Sunday sunset, we breathed a collective sigh. Now we had to walk home and face some uncomfortable truths we'd learned about ourselves.

After the Vietnam War ended, our town nobly enabled Hmong refugees to make a new home in our midst. So the war arrived at our front door, and change had found us. My father called them "Chinese," as did many men and women who knew no better. Anyone with slanty eyes was Chinese. It's decades later, and the headlines are filled with racial tensions and fears of being "invaded" by dark-skinned immigrants. The Committee on Interracial Education taught me this: It's tricky to be a human, no matter what race. It's miraculous to be humane.

Poet's Notes: Thirty-five Years

"Smile at the watercooler, but live your real life elsewhere." That's a quote from an essay by Lance Morrow which appeared in the magazine *Time.* I'd been teaching at the same college for twenty years, feeling the onset of job burnout, and Morrow's words struck a chord. Yes, I nodded, a man's life should be more than his job. Morrow's essay was addressed to his son, a father's best advice offered upon the occasion of his son's graduation. *Smile at the watercooler, but live your real life elsewhere,* I told the young faces in my classroom. Like Morrow, my advice was well-intended; I preached this doctrine over and over for several more years. It seemed like wisdom.

One day after class, I trudged back to my office, closed the door behind me, and sat slump-shouldered, staring at the wall. I'd hit my career's bottom. I was bored, withered, disengaged. Earlier that week, I'd been driving in the winter morning's darkness toward my employment, and the radio aired a news story: Researchers had determined that housecats sleep nearly two-thirds of their lives. This seemed sad to me that such a large portion of any life should be spent in dreamland, disengaged from greater possibilities of wide-eyed wakefulness. Now I realized, I'd been living like a housecat, sleeping one-third of each 24-hour day, and then smiling at the watercooler another third, biding time till I might live my real life elsewhere. Morrow's admonition no longer seemed sagacious.

"The greatest discovery of my generation" said the philosopher/psychologist William James, "is that human beings can alter their lives by altering their attitude of mind." I made a silent, solemn pact with my soul that I'd stay alert on the job to uncover at least one small opportunity for a justifiably worthwhile deed each day. When someone happened by my office door asking directions, I'd do more than mumble a reply; I'd stand and accompany them to be certain they'd arrived where they needed to go. For the man I'd shrunk into during that era of my career, this was an uncharacteristic move. I met new faces and learned deeper insight into the lives of students and colleagues I'd previously fended off at arm's length. One small act succeeded another and another, and I began not only liking the new me, but I also began liking my job. Where I'd been disengaged, I was engaged; where I'd been withering, I began to bloom. "Begin to be now what you will be here after." Those words, too, are from William James. He's talking to me. He's talking to you.

My father worked the same job (despite periodic layoffs and shutdowns) for thirty-five years, menial work in a factory, assembling window frames. He'd arrive home for supper haggard, aching in his bones and in his soul. He'd complain, and at times, he'd sit slump-shouldered at the kitchen table, starring at the wall. I think, too, he found real camaraderie among his fellow laborers. He'd bump into them in the grocery aisle on weekends; he'd stand and stall with them, joking and glad to rub shoulders with his workmates. Sometimes he'd brag about how many windows he could putty in a single day.

So, he must have carried a spark of heartfelt pride in his work. After he retired, the allure of sleeping late in the morning or taking naps in the afternoon soon lost its luster, and he spoke nostalgically about labor he maybe had once considered a meaningless grind. I don't want to believe that my father wasted his hours smiling and pretending at the watercooler, or that he numbed his mind for such a large measure of his days like a housecat drifting into idleness. At any rate, after his retirement, his attitude had changed. And so did the man.

Poet's Notes: Sentimental Value

Maybe it's possible to toss a bouquet of roses into the dustbin after the petals have withered, and to do it unceremoniously without fear of slighting someone else's well-intentioned sentiments. I'm reluctant to do so, and I don't entirely know why. I've known people who preserve flowers by drying them or pressing the blooms between pages of a fat dictionary. My wife and I had our wedding bouquet freeze-dried and protected under an expensive glass dome. After we'd paid the bill for it and brought it home, I don't think we displayed it, not even for a weekend. Where is it now? I've seen it, I think, high on one closet shelf or another over the years. What will happen to it after we're gone? Why did we fear giving up the bouquet to natural processes in the first place? Or, what's a mother to do when her son hands her a Valentine he's proudly labored over with crayons and glitter and glue? Poor Mom! After she's displayed little Jake's hand-hewn Valentine on the fridge past Fourth of July, can she justifiably part with it? If not now, when?

What to let go? What to archive for posterity? I remember my father trashing keepsakes from his family's homestead after both his parents had passed. Bundles of letters, photo albums of nameless faces and foreign places, old-fashioned draperies and woven rugs, Old World mementos, dressers and stand-alone wardrobes with hand-carved embellishments — all were thrown on a bonfire. Decades later, my wife and I spend Saturday afternoons perusing antique shops, gasping at expensive price tags. "I saw my father burn picture frames similar to these," I say, shaking my head in dismay and simultaneously knowing I've chucked in the dumpster wagon loads of objects too bothersome to hang onto, possessions likely worth hefty bags of shekels . . . someday, maybe, when my grandchildren are grown.

Not so long ago, three talented writing students of mine died in close succession. Each of the three had been enrolled in my once-a-week poetry workshop over nearly half a decade. Each had produced a solid body of work; each died entrusting the fruits of a lifetime's creative labors to my care. The manuscripts haunted me, three boxes under my desk, each labeled with a permanent marker like paupers' tombstones — Brenda, Aunda, Irvin — waiting for my next move, watching me and straining to gauge the level of my benevolence or the shabbiness of my neglect.

And what's to become of what I leave behind? Now that I need reading glasses and ads for hearing-aids arrive in my mail, I wake at night and wonder. So much of what I've gathered — boat, cars, tools — these can all be born again as secondhand bargains, trucked away by The Salvation Army. But what about my manuscripts, and where will the several dozen hardback notebooks I've carried close to me constantly for so many years . . . where will they go when I'm gone? Those pages are the voice of a man's innermost joys and fears and longings. Those pages are a portrait of my soul. The old saying, "You can't take it with you," is easy enough to bear, but wouldn't you like to depart knowing you've bequeathed to your grandchildren something more than ashes and cash?

My mother took it upon herself to archive boxes and boxes of birthday cards, grade reports, and any scrap of paper mentioning her children's names. It became a burden for her, and her children never overtly acknowledged her loving intentions. I've rummaged through the debris. Pages of grade school addition and subtraction seem like someone else's right and wrong answers, even though it's my name penciled at the heading. I did rediscover a spiral notebook of poems I'd composed in junior high — bawdy, crude, rhyming parodies of early Sixties rock ballads. They made me laugh. The notebook sits on a shelf in my office now. I just can't find it in me to throw it away.

Poet's Notes: Someone Needs to Keep Track

Lucky for me, I married a woman who keeps track of things. She manages our bank accounts, our investments, our taxes. She also keeps track of our kids' birthdays, and she'll issue little prompts to rescue me from forgetting our wedding anniversary or to remind me I've got a dental checkup next week. "Where's that red coat of mine?" I'll ask when cold winds begin to blow, and she'll point me toward the particular closet where the coat has been hanging all along, waiting for my return. Or I'll say, "Do you remember that hotel in Wyoming with the balcony overlooking the hot springs . . . how we sat up till almost sunrise laughing and talking and watching the stars?" "That was in Canada," she'll respond. I don't argue; her memory is more reliable than mine.

My mother faithfully kept a journal, a "Year Book." These little hardcover books weren't appointment books, exactly, or diaries, or account ledgers; they were blank pages she used as she saw fit. Even as a kid, I wondered why she bothered to record each day's weather and expenses, but so little else. One page every day, year after year, she'd sit at the kitchen table and write: "Six inches of snow this morning. Cold. Lots of wind. $23.78 for groceries. $9 for gas. No mail."

Now, as an older person, I scan her daily statistics and read between the lines. More important than the facts of each day was the act of keeping track, of contributing her particular skills to hold our family intact. Like so many moms in the 1950s, she was what we now call a "stay-at-home" mom. Back then, the term was "housewife," which sounds like she was married to the house, and in some ways that may be true. Amidst the turbulence of bickering children and her husband's layoffs and job changes, she held us together in her own way, day by day tracking our survival, which at times must surely have seemed less than likely.

In a backhanded manner, she was writing about herself, inadvertently revealing who she was in syllables she might not have guessed. Within the camouflage of her stats lies hidden the fact of her wish to contribute, to be of value, to record where we'd landed at the close of each day in hope of finding a way forward. In hindsight, I think both my parents were often overwhelmed and felt helpless in the face of unsteady wages and never-ending bills. How to keep going? This was the conundrum. *The rich get richer,* my father would shake his head. *Yeah,* Mom would reply, *and the poor get nothin'.* My father's only plan was to rise and dress when he heard the shift whistle beckoning. My mother's strategy was to cook and clean and keep track of the cost of groceries and gas.

Mom had a "pocketbook" hanging on a hook in the hall, but I doubt she ever needed more than a coin purse. She learned to drive, but didn't practice the skill for so long she one day claimed to have forgotten how. Dad cashed his paychecks at the grocery store and folded dollar bills in his wallet carefully, daily thumbing through the thin wad to count what was left. And did I mention that some nights I'd lie in bed beside my brothers and listen to our parents washing and drying dishes, singing "I Wanna Be a Cowboy's Sweetheart," Mom carrying the melody, Dad harmonizing, both yodeling the chorus? Mom's scribbling never included details of these more expressive scenarios. So I've grown up with a compulsion to write this down. Somebody needs to keep track.

Poet's Notes: The Pillow

The "talking cure." The name rings flat, an awkward combination of words, an inadequate attempt to name what takes place in a therapist's office. So much talk, talk, talk in this world of deafening nonsense. Yet, I'd like to talk about it, now, with you, dear therapist, assuming two-hundred dollars an hour will buy a revelation, will unlock secrets I've stashed, then forgotten where, forgotten why. I've witnessed how the talking cure can make a blind man see; I'll testify, too, how the talking cure may merely gather more darkness where what's needed is increased light. "More light! More light!" said Goethe on his deathbed. Did he die with important things to say left unsaid?

The biggest, bad-boy conundrum humankind has ever faced: How blind are we to the world around us? And worse, how blind are we to ourselves? I've been reading about "naïve realism," the supposition that each of us believes he perceives the world accurately, and in doing so he is self-deceived. We stand with our backs to the fire, watching shadows dance on the walls of Plato's Cave. Or, we are peeking at reality through a keyhole, afraid to open the door. Nor can our "sense of self" be trusted; we are prone to painting ourselves in a flattering light, likely to highlight characteristics we favor while obfuscating darker forces in us we'd rather conceal. It's a make-up job every morning, standing in front of the mirror, constructing again — for myself especially — the face of an illusion I've dreamed.

Sorry if the notions above twang a foreboding chord. We needn't push too far; let's simply concede to our frailties and self-deceptions, and let's march onward as each sunrise succeeds the last one. Sylvia Plath spent long, sleepless hours stripping her psyche, as if peeling back the layers of an onion. What did she find, I wonder? Or what was she looking for and failed to discover? We can only guess answers to these questions, but we know for certain how that sad story ends. I, for one, am still struggling with this: How to locate the balance between craving self-knowledge and illumination and the wisdom to step back now and again to catch my breath, to let my heart rest?

Think of two primitive souls walking across the savanna, our ancient ancestors in search of food and shelter. Both men suddenly spy movement in the tall grass. Maybe it's just a stray breath of wind. Maybe it's a hungry tiger. One man wants to get a better look and moves forward. The other man steps back, slowly. Which would evolution favor? Which man's genes were passed along to reach me and you? Which man's bones were scattered in tiger scat? It's not a justifiable analogy in some ways, but stealthy psychic/emotional tigers can indeed chew you up and digest your unsuspecting eyeballs. A man needs to know when to tell his therapist to stop pushing onward. The patient needs to retreat, slowly, in search of a place to hide, in search of a weapon to protect him from memory's sharp bite.

The incident depicted in the poem "The Pillow" may be a fictional tale, maybe not. I just didn't like the look on the therapist's face when he handed over the pillow. Was he enjoying his patient's pain and discomfort? Was he drunk with a sense of power over a man who'd fallen injured along the trail? Was he pouncing like a tiger? All I know is that when I threw the pillow back at him, he'd lost his advantage. I needed to defend my mother, as I always had, even though she was dead and gone.

Okay, if that's what the therapist intended, he wins. It worked.

Poet's Notes: Ghosting Home

      As a middle-child, I felt largely overlooked for most of my life. No surprises there, eh? Middle children are prone to feeling like outsiders. I've no intention to sound self-pitying; oldest and youngest children must bear separate challenges of their own station, and so do all siblings in between. Yet . . . I'm amused to have just written the sentence above. How like a middle-child to concede his pain as not so important, really. And what a strange place to begin this little reflection on the poem "Ghosting Home." Why begin here?

      When I was a kid, I liked to dismantle castoff alarm clocks. I'd unscrew the housing to look inside at the gears and springs and rocker arms, and I'd marvel at the machine's complexities. This felt like I was unlocking important secrets, especially when I prodded one gear to move another and sometimes the whole contraption came alive. I find a similar thrill in writing a poem; the act of penning a poem can reveal the complexities of what makes me tick. Self-knowledge feels good some days and other days painful. Is it wise to look inside? "Know thyself," said Socrates. "The truth will set you free" — these words were inscribed over the doors of my college when I was an undergrad, and I wondered what, exactly, could that mean? "For much wisdom is much grief, and he who increases his knowledge increases his sorrow." Those are the words of King Solomon (Ecclesiastes 1:18), and some say he was the wisest man ever. Do you see the conflict here? How can the truth set us free and also cause us pain? In trying to discover how the alarm clock kept time, I also discovered my own limitations. I couldn't fix what was broken. At times, I'd disassemble the mechanism too far, and the tiny gears lay separated from the whole, a senseless jumble.

      "Feels good to get that off my chest," we say. We've made a lasting and popular metaphor for our emotional-psychic troubles; we call them our "burden," and we "carry" them like "baggage." After finishing a poem, I feel as if I'd abandoned a box-load of heavy rocks along the roadside. I also know I'll likely drive away into the sunset seeking even more inventive discord. Sorry, does "seeking even more inventive discord" sound snarky? Ask yourself this: Do you know anyone on this wide wonderful planet who holds the keys to Nirvana for good and forever? It's another facet of the human condition that we go through eras of calm and bouts of chaos, isn't it? This truth sets me free to see more clearly who I am. This wisdom fills me with sorrow. This wisdom fills me with mirth.

      What have you hidden from others, especially the nearest and dearest? What have you hidden from yourself? Well, I love a good mystery, and I was short on clues and plenty curious for years as to why I felt so torn apart whenever I crossed the continent to visit the home-place and try once again to connect with family. In setting to the page the poem "Ghosting Home," I discovered wisdom I'd never spoken before, and I found what I'd kept hidden from myself most of all. Sure, I'd always been an alien to my family, at least I believed it so, but I'd also become an alien to the workings of my own heart. Can you locate the particular line?

Poet's Notes: Listening

I was born and raised in the Midwest and never saw the ocean until I was out of high school. I still stand in awe whenever I've stopped to hear the surf pounding. The rhythm of the waves, the relentless crashing roar, the far-off horizon — transport my thoughts to that high place where the best poems await discovery, those rare moments of insightful transcendence where a man can glimpse his own small and mysterious place amidst the greatness and grandeur of creation.

For many years I taught writing workshops at Coos Bay, Oregon, and I fell in love with Oregon's rocky, time-sculpted coastline. I'd ask the students to do a writing exercise in which we'd each wander alone on the beach in search of an object small enough to hold in one hand — a shell, a bone, a sea-worn wood chip, a shiny stone. *Just listen for something calling,* I'd say. We'd carry our small treasures back to the classroom, and we'd sit with them in silence until we heard what each had to say, which is pretty much how I wrote the poem "Listening." One day I climbed trails along the dunes and up into the high bluffs overlooking the vast grey-blue. I caught a pebble inside my shoe. Or did the pebble catch me? If you listen intently enough, there's a lesson in every small thing.

In Mary Oliver's fine poem, "The Summer Day," she says: "I don't know, exactly, what a prayer is. / I do know how to pay attention . . . ." My poem "Listening" is a sort of prayer on my 60th birthday, but moreover it's a poem that pays attention to the little things, small voices which are often the echoes of larger implications. Some people see the big picture; others see the details. Poets need to see both. My best poems focus first on something small, a detail commanding my attention, insisting I listen to what it has to say. It's true that sometimes we can't see the forest for the trees, which is to say we are blinded to the larger meaning of things if we are hyper-focused on specifics alone. On the other hand, we'll never fully comprehend larger meanings if we don't honor each particular as an indispensable part of the whole. A forest is composed of individual trees. A chorus consists of many small voices.

Speaking of small voices . . . have you heard your own? That "still, small voice" whispering in your ear . . . have you heard it? Are you listening? What is that voice? Well, I can't pretend to know for certain, but I suspect each of us is born with an Old Wise Person who rides along with us in our heads and knows our hearts better than we do. That Old Wise Person is the still, small voice asking us — at times begging us! — to be true to ourselves, to set out on the path we were born to follow, to fan the embers of passion, to fill our days with gusto, to discover our personal wellsprings of joy. In my poems, I lean close and pay attention; I listen to the still, small voice whispering in my ear.

As I've aged, my Old Wise Person has gone hoarse with laughter to witness my wrong turns and stumbles. But he's hung on for the ride these many years; he spurs me this way and that, and I've learned to let him point the way. My parents were deeply flawed, and yet I knew they loved me. This is the wisdom my Old Wise Person whispered to me early on. I am no less flawed than my parents. This is true of all of us. Oh! Why has it taken so long for my ears to hear my Old Wise Person's most important lessons!

"The end of all our exploring," wrote T. S. Eliot, "will be to arrive where we started and know the place for the first time." I had a vivid dream one troubled night in which I walked as a

child again, wandering in gut-twisting darkness, anxious, alone, swallowing my panic and pushing myself, step by step, blindly forward. Then I bumped into a set of grown-up legs, and when I looked up, I was also the man reaching down to take my hand. *It's okay,* he said, *you turn out to be me.* I woke and knew I'd arrived where I'd started. I'd journeyed the full circle.

Despite so many diversions and distractions, despite the chaos and uncertainty of my early years, I would become the person I was meant to be. The Old Wise Person in me knew it all along.

Listen. Who are you? Who are you meant to be?

Questions for Further Reflection and Discussion

Some Memories Never Leave

1.) What are your favorite family stories? Do other family members tell these stories differently? How factually accurate are these stories? What has been embellished? What has been deleted?

2.) Can you think of particular moments in your experience that became "the music of your heart"? In what ways were those moments important in shaping who you are?

3.) Can you imagine how your life might have unfolded differently had you been born elsewhere and under vastly different circumstances? Would you still be the same person inside, or might differing circumstances have altered who you are inside and how you present yourself to the world?

4.) Think of your favorite books or movies. What stories do they tell? Have the stories in these books or movies added to your sense of who you are or to the story you tell yourself about who you are?

Prompt: Write about one of your earliest childhood memories. What event comes to mind? Did this event foretell the sort of person you've become?

Buzz-Cut Saturdays

1.) What is the "rhythm" of your life? How has the rhythm of your life changed over time?

2.) What are the important milestones in your life? How have these moments shaped who you are today? Think past obvious milestones such as marriage, giving birth to a child, or completing school. What smaller or more mundane events also shaped you in important ways?

3.) The young boy in the poem "Buzz-Cut Saturdays" has been influenced by his father's favorite metaphor — the mythical hero-soldier. What metaphors for right conduct did your parents or others offer to you? How did these metaphors affect your outlook on life?

4.) Can you love someone and feel unsuccessful in expressing your love? Some thinkers have described different love "languages" by which we try to show love or by which we feel love from others. (See: *5 Love Languages* by Gary Chapman.) How do you show love to others? What are the best ways for others to show love to you?

Prompt: Write about a particular moment when you felt loved. What specific gestures gave you that impression?

Bull-Headed

1.) Why do kids ask, "What's your favorite animal?" How might a person's choice of favorite animal reflect upon that person's character?

2.) Folk stories and mythologies often use animals to illustrate right and wrong conduct for humans. (See: *The Power of Myth* by Joseph Campbell.) What lessons do you learn from nature? Can you name particular plants or animals that have been your teachers? How so?

3.) "The human condition" — What does that phrase mean to you? As a species, are we similar to one another, or dissimilar? How are you unique? How are you like everyone else?

4.) How is the poem "Bull-Headed" a praise poem?

Prompt: Think of an animal you admire or enjoy. Focus on a single encounter. Write about what lessons that animal might teach you.

Working on My Words

1.) Have you discovered your calling? How did this discovery happen? If you haven't discovered your calling yet, can you name a close acquaintance who has? How do you know this person has discovered his or her calling? How does he or she show it?

2.) Are people born to their calling, or do people choose their calling? Or, do the events of a person's life lead them inexorably toward one calling or another?

3.) Read "In the Waiting Room" by Elizabeth Bishop. She writes: "But I felt; you are an I, / you are an 'Elizabeth,' / you are one of them." Can you think of a moment in your experience when you felt the fact of your own existence? What words might you use to describe that experience?

4.) "Follow your bliss." — What do these words mean? Is this always good advice? If not, how so? (See: *The Hero with a Thousand Faces* by Joseph Campbell.)

Prompt: Write about the day you discovered your calling. Inside and outside, what were the signals?

She Didn't Like What She Didn't Know

1.) Of the five physical senses — taste, touch, smell, hearing, sight — which are your strongest? Do you experience these senses more strongly than the average person? How do you know? Were you born with these heightened senses, or did these senses increase in you as you gained experience over time?

2.) What sort of non-physical senses do you experience? When do you have your best hunches? When have you experienced knowing something intuitively? Can you trust your intuition? Can intuition mislead you?

3.) Have you experienced a "Eureka!" moment? Some thinkers advise — when we are tackling a seemingly unsolvable puzzle — that we put it aside and let our unconscious work on it. "Sleep on it," we say. (See: *The Creative Spirit* by Goleman, Kaufman, and Ray.) Have you experienced new insights into a problem by letting it go?

4.) Read the poem "The Red Wheelbarrow" by William Carlos Williams. This is a poem some people love to hate, just like some people love to hate modern art. What are your reactions upon first reading the poem? We say, "A picture is worth a thousand words." Can we say the same for an image, or a "word-picture"?

Prompt: Rummage awhile in your junk-drawer or storage closet. What one object calls to you, makes you curious? Write about that object. Be sure to describe it in detail. What does that object tell us about who you are?

"Bath Time!"

1.) What joys did you experience as a child? What tragedies? How have these events colored your outlook toward human relationships? Toward nature? Toward yourself?

2.) How might religion "suffocate" a person? What messages might be conveyed by employing metaphors like "soiled with sin" or "dirty as worms"?

3.) In the poem "Bath Time!" what does the narrator mean when he says, "Hard to believe / Jehovah's spite"? Is "spite" the right word to use? This poem relies on ironies. Can you list them?

4.) In the poem "Bath Time!" how does the Narrator romanticize nature? When does sentiment become overly sentimental? Can we be realistically nostalgic? Nature lovers are prone to romanticize the natural world. In this romanticized frame of mind, how can nature lovers be insightful? How might they be blinded?

Prompt: Write about a moment when you felt especially connected to the natural world. Have you ever been skinny-dipping? Have you ever walked barefoot in the mud? Have you ever looked closely at the grasshopper clinging to your shirt sleeve?

Washday, Everyday

1.) Some dreamers make purposeful efforts toward actualizing their dreams, while other dreamers wait for good fortune to knock at their door. Can you identify an element of both of these in your own plans for the future? Are you more one type of dreamer than the other?

2.) Some people avoid talking about their aspirations for fear others will laugh or criticize. Some people avoid talking about their aspirations for fear telling too much will jinx the outcome. What other reasons might people have to stay quiet?

3.) What is the difference between being content with one's situation or being resigned to the way things are? How does a person display contentment? How does a person display resignation?

4.) It's a popular notion these days to think that each of us must take care of himself before he can take care of others. In the poem "Washday, Everyday," how would the mother view that notion?

Prompt: Write about a man or a woman doing hard physical labor. What details and specifics best describe this person at work? How do his/her actions reveal his/her attitudes?

Seim's Bottle Gas

1.) In your own family, are you a middle child, youngest, oldest, or somewhere between? How has birth order affected you? How has it affected your siblings? What might be the advantages or disadvantages of being an only child? What might be upsides or downsides of having multiple siblings?

2.) It's a common admonishment that parents shouldn't favor one child over another. Is it possible for parents to distribute their affections equally? How? Is it possible for parents to treat their children differently and still maintain a sense of fairness and equal treatment? How?

3.) Can you recall moments in your childhood when you felt your parents had singled you out for special attention and care? Was it a conscious decision on your parents' part, or did it just happen?

4.) What attitudes or values did you learn from your parents? Which of these hand-me-down attitudes or values do you still carry with you today? Which have you since rejected or discarded? Why?

Prompt: Write about visiting a parent's workplace. What did you see? What did you learn?

Slugs (1963)

1.) Is it possible, as William James said, to alter your life by altering your attitude of mind? Can you think of times when this has worked for you? Can you think of people who seem stuck in their lives and stuck in their attitudes of mind?

2.) In the poem "Slugs," what lessons does the boy learn from his father? Is the father leading his son astray? We say, "The road to Hell is paved with good intentions." Are the father's actions forgivable because his intentions are benevolent toward his son? Why or why not?

3.) What's the line between serious crime and petty crime? Who defines the difference? How does justice for a serious crime differ from justice for a petty crime?

4.) In the poem "Slugs," how do you think the father would explain or justify his actions? How does the father's "attitude of mind" help him justify his actions? How would the boy justify his own actions?

Prompt: Write about someone you knew who led you astray. How did you succumb to his/her influence? What were the consequences?

You Be Good

1.) What words of advice have your parents given you? Where did your parents learn these lessons they wanted to teach you? If you are a parent, what advice have you offered your children? Where or when or how did you come upon these lessons you feel are worth passing on to your children?

2.) How would the father in the poem "You Be Good" define "good"? According to the father, what characterizes a "good" man?

3.) What's the value of a job? Beyond wages, what rewards can a job provide?

4.) In the midst of personal difficulties, how might it be good advice to "just keep going"? How might this advice be short-sighted?

Prompt: Write about a pet phrase or words of advice a parent offered to you over and over. Was this advice worthwhile, or not? What does a parent's advice say about his/her character?

"Holy Cow!"

1.) Children will admonish one another not to use "bad" words. Why are some words considered "bad"? Who decides?

2.) American English is rich with regional dialects. "Holy cow!" for instance, is an expression common in the Midwest and not so common in other regions. What are particular phrases, expressions, exclamations, or word variations common to your region?

3.) Idiolect is the word we use to describe individual differences in language usage. Your idiolect may be comprised of words you have inadvertently twisted or mispronounced. Can you think of examples?

4.) What is the difference between poetry and prose? Is this an important distinction? Why or why not? Should poetry be read aloud differently than prose? How so? Try reading a poem as if it were prose. Try reading a prose paragraph as if it were poetry. (See Henry Taylor's poem "One Morning Shoeing Horses" for an interesting exploration of the fine line between what sounds like poetry and what sounds like prose.)

Prompt: Write about curse words or exclamations you spoke as a child. Think about a particular situation when you employed one of these words or exclamations passionately. What was the outcome?

Great Aunt Ida's Last Christmas

1.) In the poem "Great Aunt Ida's Last Christmas," what is the father's attitude toward his Aunt Ida? What is Aunt Ida's attitude toward everyone else in the poem? What is the narrator's attitude toward his father? Toward Great Aunt Ida?

2.) Some changes are more difficult than others. Great Aunt Ida is facing one sort of difficulty with change, and the father is facing another sort of difficulty with change. Can you describe the difficulties each is facing?

3.) Decades before the digital revolution, some thinkers predicted that humans would struggle more and more with change, and the pace of change itself would accelerate. (See: *Future Shock* by Alvin Toffler.) How has change affected your life? What challenges have you faced in keeping pace with change?

4.) "The more things change, the more they stay the same." Can you think of examples of this irony in your own life? Is change inevitable? Is it necessary? What changes are "good" changes, and what changes are "not so good"? Does anything not change? If so, what?

Prompt: Write about an older person set in his/her ways. Describe events in which this person clearly demonstrates his/her resistance to change.

How We Survived the Cuban Missile Crisis

1.) The 1950s and 60s were scary years to be a kid. Every era is fraught with impending dangers. In your lifetime, what world events or natural disasters troubled you? Which were real dangers? Which were imagined?

2.) "Life goes on," we say after tragedy or disaster, "and you must go on, too." Is this valid advice for all circumstances? Under what circumstances might this be worthwhile advice? Under what circumstances might this advice be less worthwhile?

3.) Why don't our evening newscasts and newspapers contain more good news? Is bad news more vital or interesting than good news?

4.) In a crisis, how should parents prepare their children? In the poem "How We Survived the Cuban Missile Crisis," how might the parents have done better?

Prompt: Think about a day you and your family prepared for a disaster. Write about your family's preparations. Was the disaster real, or was it imagined? What was the outcome?

The Cold War at Home

1.) During the 1950s and 60s, the United States and the Soviet Union were engaged in the Cold War. What characterizes a "cold" war? How can there be a Cold War at home?

2.) In the poem "The Cold War at Home," why does the boy put himself in the middle? Is he helping the situation? Or is he making things worse?

3.) In the poem, when the Boy says he built a bomb shelter in his head, what does he mean?

4.) In what ways might the Boy have responded differently when his parents quarreled?

Prompt: Write about a situation where you found yourself haplessly mediating a dispute between two warring parties. Why were you in the middle? What was the outcome?

Peace

1.) "You just can't understand unless you've been there." Can you think of situations in which this notion is true? Can a man truly understand what it's like to be a woman? Can a woman truly understand what it's like to be a man? Can you understand what it's like to be poor if you've never been poor?

2.) Does it do any good to ponder the "unknown self" — the fourth quadrant of the Johari Window?

3.) How do you think you might react in combat? Can you think of situations in which you felt extreme pressure and stress? How did you react? Were you surprised?

4.) Pause for a moment to think about the most important people in your life. How much do you know about their lives before you came along? What stories might they be withholding?

Prompt: Write a poem, story, or essay titled "You Can't Understand." What is it you understand about the particular event in question that no one else can understand?

Broke

1.) What is a "good" man? What is a "good" woman? Do you see yourself as a "good" person? By what standards do you make this assessment of yourself?

2.) Is it necessary that we have a welfare system by which people in need can receive public assistance? Why, or why not?

3.) Why do people seek public assistance? Are they unable to make ends meet because of character flaws? Or, are they unable to make ends meet due to circumstance beyond their control?

4.) In the poem "Broke," the father was broke financially, but the poem implies that he was also broken in some other way. Why did the father feel ashamed to ask for public assistance?

Prompt: Write about a specific situation in which you found it difficult or impossible to ask for help. Did you finally struggle past your reluctance? How did others respond to your summons?

The Test

1.) "Humankind," said T. S. Eliot, "cannot bear very much reality." Is this true? Why, or why not? Can you name examples of things you would rather not know or rather not remember?

2.) "You are unaware of how unaware you are," writes David McRaney. Can you give examples of memories you've conflated? Why do you suppose you've conflated these memories? Have you ever conflated a memory and convinced yourself it was true? (See: *You Are Not So Smart* by David McRaney.)

3.) "Not everything that counts can be counted," Einstein said. Can you think of examples to illustrate what that quote means?

4.) Do you agree or disagree with the notion that truth may be more than facts alone might reveal? Can there be truth without facts? Can you give examples of misleading facts?

Prompt: Write about a memory you've likely embellished or conflated. Let the reader "see" how this memory has morphed over time.

Things Got Worse

1.) Think of a relationship which has changed over time. Can you point to specific events which altered this relationship? Or did the relationship change slowly, almost invisibly, over time?

2.) When you were young, to what extent did you look up to your parents or older siblings? If they seemed awesome and god-like, how did these impressions change? Are there children, now, looking up to you? What do they see?

3.) The notion of "fabulous reality" encourages us to apprehend and appreciate the extraordinary nature of all things ordinary. Look around: How is your reality "fabulous"? Can you cite examples? (See: *Telling Writing* by Ken Macrorie.)

4.) "Our world is colorless and boring only because we are blind." Do you agree or disagree? Some people say they enjoy living uneventful lives. How can this be?

Prompt: Write about a specific event which altered a significant relationship. How did the relationship change? What were the most revealing clues?

Wesley's Playland

1.) Do you have a devil on one shoulder and an angel on the other? Have you felt an inner primitive urge to walk on the "wild side"? How have you responded to that urge?

2.) "Be careful when casting out your demons that you don't throw away the best of yourself," wrote Friedrich Nietzsche. What can these words mean?

3.) "Nothing human is alien to me," wrote the Roman playwright Terence. How might this notion affect the administration of justice?   Are there no limits to empathy?

4.) In your experience, how have your friends influenced you?   Can you name a friend who has been a bad influence? How did you befriend that person in the first place?

Prompt: Have you been cautioned not to be led astray by a bad influence? What attracted you to that influence? Write about the debate between the angel on your one shoulder and the devil on the other.

Weasel Shit

1.) Look up the term "mondegreen." Our mother complained about her varicose veins; we misheard her words and thought she said, "very close veins." Can you think of instances when you've misheard a word or phrase? How did you discover your error?

2.) Can you think of a situation in which you ended up laughing at yourself? Why might this be a valuable skill?

3.) What's the difference between laughing at someone and laughing with someone? When is self-deprecating humor useful? When does it fall flat?

4.) Can you remember particular moments in a movie or TV show that made you laugh aloud? Why did you laugh?

Prompt: Can you think of a particular song or saying which you misheard? Write about how your twisted version made sense to you.

Lewis and Clark the Hard Way

1.) Is it possible to be a good learner but not a very good student? What are the characteristics of a good learner? What are the characteristics of a good student?

2.) How do adventure stories "capture" our imaginations? What are the elements of an enjoyable adventure story? (See: *The Hero with Ten Thousand Faces* by Joseph Campbell.)

3.) If you could design the perfect school, how would it differ from most schools today?

4.) What are the strengths and weaknesses of being a realist? What are the strengths and weaknesses of being an idealist? Are you more of a realist, or more of an idealist? Why do you think so?

Prompt: Who was your childhood hero? Why? How did your impression of this person change over time? What did your original infatuation tell you about your hopes and dreams? Write about this complicated relationship. Can you find humor in all this?

Murder

1.) "Nothing can shield us from the greater world and darker realities inevitably knocking at our door." Do you agree or disagree? Why?

2.) "Ignorance is bliss." What is the value of this notion? What are its limitations? "The truth will set you free." What is the value of this opposite notion? What are its limitations?

3.) Why do onlookers gather at the scene of a crime? Why do tabloid newspapers sensationalize crime? Why do people read sensationalized crime stories?

4.) Why do people gossip?

Prompt: Write about a specific moment which opened your eyes. What were the details of the situation? How did your perception of yourself and your world change?

Goodbye, Wesley

1.) In novels or movies, what makes fictional characters seem real?

2.) We say, "Actions speak louder than words." How do writers use actions to characterize people? Can you think of an example from a favorite book or movie?

3.) "Do I contradict myself?" wrote Walt Whitman, "Very well, then I contradict myself, / (I am large, I contain multitudes.)" What might these words mean? Can you identify contradictory aspects of your own character? How do you justify these contradictions?

4.) How do best friends become friends in the first place? Why do friends grow apart? How is intimacy between friends different from intimacy between lovers?

Prompt: Write about a childhood friend. What adventures did you and this friend have? How did you become friends? How did you grow apart?

Let's Hope This Thing Blows Over Soon

1.) Read Wilfred Owen's poem "Dulce et Decorum Est." "How sweet and noble to die for one's homeland." — How might someone defend the truth of this statement? Why does Owen call it "the old lie"?

2.) "Those who cannot remember the past are condemned to repeat it," wrote George Santayana. "I've got news for Mr. Santayana," responded Kurt Vonnegut, "we're doomed to repeat the past no matter what. That's what it is to be alive." What are your thoughts concerning Santayana's words and Vonnegut's response?

3.) How has warfare changed over time? What hasn't changed? Will there ever be an end to war? (Santayana also wrote: "Only the dead have seen the end of war.")

4.) In the poem "Let's Hope This Thing Blows over Soon," the father puts his arm around his son's shoulders and says, "Let's hope this thing blows over soon." What did the father intend to communicate by his actions and his words? How did the boy respond?

Prompt: Write about a moral dilemma, a situation in which you grappled with right and wrong action. What was the issue? How did you finally decide what to do?

Hitchhiker

1.) What shapes your life? Fate? Luck? Divine design? Willpower? Have you ever felt "anointed" in some predestined way, or "dusted with magic"? In your autobiography, what chains of events are easily attributed to cause and effect? What random events played a hand? Are you surprised to be who you are? Why, or why not?

2.) What does it mean to "live mythically"? Have you ever felt like you were watching yourself as a character in the story of your own life? In novels and plays, the plot most often progresses along a "narrative arc" — an identifiable theme threading through the beginning, middle, and end. Can you identify a narrative arc in your own life?

3.) "Much like we grow out of one pair of shoes into the next, we outgrow our childhood consciousness into levels increasingly more expansive and mature." Do you agree, or disagree? What characterizes a "childhood consciousness"? What does it mean to "outgrow" that consciousness? How would you describe that transformation? How did this transformation happen for you?

4.) Do you have a calling? What are your passions? Fill in this blank: I am a born_____. The Hero, The Soldier, The Healer, The Priest, The Scholar, The Scribe, The Prophet, The Trickster, The Hunter, The Athlete, The Artist — who are you? Why?

Prompt: Write about a "magical" moment — an incident in which you were inexplicably spared harm, or an incident in which the stars seemed mysteriously aligned in your favor.

Let's Get Stupid

1.) Are depictions of the 60s "Love Generation" often romanticized? If you aren't old enough to have lived through that era, talk to someone who has. Ask them what was pleasurable about those years and what was less than pleasurable. How about the military draft and the nightly body counts on TV newscasts? How about drug addiction, drug overdose, and drug-related deaths? "Hindsight is 20-20," we say. Is it? Or do we remember things as we want them to be more than how they really were?

2.) Drug abuse seems to be ever on the rise. What's the attraction?   In the poem "Let's Get Stupid," what motivates the boys to get high?

3.) How might drugs help a person cope with stress? With depression? How might drugs worsen the problem?

4.) In what ways can our language reveal who we are? Can our choice of words expose our unrecognized attitudes and assumptions?   What attitudes and assumptions are revealed in the words "Let's get stupid"?

Prompt: Write about doing something stupid, something you thought might be a good idea but turned out badly. Did anyone caution you beforehand? Why didn't you heed that caution?

Action

1.) We say, "Action speaks louder than words." Is this always true? Can inaction also be a strategy? Can silence be a strategy?

2.) The more we boldly announce our plans, the less likely we will achieve them. This notion seems counterintuitive, but why might it be true? If this notion is true, what does it teach us about human behavior?

3.) Read "The Hollow Men" by T. S. Eliot. "Between the idea / And the reality / Between the motion / And the act / Falls the Shadow." What do these words mean? Might Eliot's view of human nature be called satirical? Why, or why not?

4.) Are you motivated intrinsically or extrinsically? What spurs you into action? What forces stop you from acting?

Prompt: Write about plans you made and failed to get started. How might your history have changed (for better or for worse) if you had followed through on your plans?

Kissing

1.) "Love makes fools of us all." How has your experience of love or romance been both humorous and humiliating?

2.) "I've looked at love from both sides now." How would you define "both sides"? Are there more sides?

3.) What are our "biological imperatives"? How much are we controlled by our hormones? How much are our "powers of reason" influenced by chemicals in the brain — dopamine, serotonin, endorphins, oxytocin, etc.?

4.) We talk about the "battle of the sexes." How would you define that battle? What makes a man or a woman attractive?

Prompt: Write a poem, or story, or essay titled "Love Makes Fools of Us All." Use your own experience to illustrate the title.

You Don't Sound So Good

1.) What actions or what words do you use to show your love? By what actions or words do you want others to show love to you? How do different people show love differently?

2.) What do the words "unspoken love" mean to you?

3.) What do the words "tough love" mean to you? What is a "toxic" relationship?

4.) If you were near your last few hours on earth, what would you want to hear from your loved ones?

Prompt: Write about a situation in which you wanted to express love or gratitude or appreciation, and you failed to speak. Did you attempt to communicate your sentiments by some other means?

Change Finds My Hometown

1.) In the poem, "Change Finds My Hometown," why is the father upset about immigrants moving into his town? Why is the mother upset? What does the sister mean when she says, "The world is changing and won't stop"?

2.) What was the "counter-culture" movement of the 1960s?   What social and political changes did the counter-culture advocate?

3.) What social and political changes did the Civil Rights Movement of the 1950s and 1960s advocate? How did people react?

4.) What social changes have occurred in the last two or three decades? How did people react? Why do some people advocate change? Why do some people fear change?

Prompt: Write about a moment when you struggled to accept unavoidable change. Were you afraid of the changes? Why were the changes difficult to accept? Who favored the changes? Why?

Thirty-five Years

1.) Why might it be virtuous to keep the same job for a long time? Why might it not be such a good idea?

2.) "Smile at the watercooler, but live your real life elsewhere." What do these words mean? Think of a job you've held; how engaged or disengaged were you? What caused you to engage? What caused you to disengage?

3.) In the poem "Thirty-Five Years," why is the father dissatisfied with his retirement? How does he express his dissatisfaction? What is the narrator's attitude toward his father?

4.) What are your plans and dreams for retirement? How might your plans change?

Prompt: Write about your worst job ever. How did you get the job in the first place? What went wrong? How might you have made the job more tolerable? What did you learn?

Sentimental Value

1.) How do you define "sentimental value"? What things are worth hanging onto? Why?

2.) We say, "You can't take it with you." How do you want people to remember you? What will be your "legacy"? What's to become of what you leave behind?

3.) In the poem, "Sentimental Value," why does the mother take it upon herself to archive family mementos? How do her children respond to their mother's efforts? Why?

4.) Why do some items gain material value over time? Why do some items gain sentimental value over time? What's the difference?

Prompt: Write about a particular item you've imbued with sentimental value. Why is this item important? How does this item represent what you value most? Can you imagine losing this item?

Someone Needs to Keep Track

1.) In the poem "Someone Needs to Keep Track," the mother keeps a daily journal. What value might these journals be to the family? What value might these journals be to a sociologist? To a historian? To a psychologist? To a visitor from outer space?

2.) Why does the mother in the poem take it upon herself to keep her daily records? Why does she think these records are of value to the family? How are these records of value to her?

3.) Several poems in *Someday I'd Write This Down* portray marriage in the 1950s and 60s. How have marriage relationships changed since then? How much hasn't changed?

4.) In the digital age, we are capable of storing massive amounts of data. What can data tell us about our lives? What can't data tell us?

Prompt: Compose an imaginary journal entry written by a loved one. What might he or she have to say? In selecting the content of the entry, how can you reveal the imagined writer's character?

The Pillow

1.) In the poem "The Pillow," why does the narrator distrust the therapist? What is the therapist trying to accomplish?

2.) How can talking be a cure?

3.) Was the therapy session a success, or not? Does the narrator benefit from this therapy? Does he learn anything new?

4.) Generally, introspection is held to be worthwhile, but is it possible to go too far? How so? Can you think of an example? Why are some people more introspective than others?

Prompt: Write about a situation in which someone tried to counsel you but gave you misguided advice. How was their advice intended to help? How did you know the advice was misguided?

Ghosting Home

1.) Are you an only child? Middle child? Youngest? Oldest? How has your position in the family structure affected your relationship with your parents?

2.) In the poem "Ghosting Home," how does the narrator react to his father's decline? In the final line of the poem, what does the narrator "know"?

3.) "For much wisdom is much grief, and he who increases his knowledge increases his sorrow." — What do these words mean? "The truth will set you free." — What do these words mean? Do the two quotes contradict one another? Why or why not?

4.) Have you ever experienced "the relentless oh, oh, oh" of your astounded soul? What were the circumstances? What was the outcome?

Prompt: Write about witnessing a loved one's mental or physical decline. Be specific and detailed. Was the decline difficult to witness, or not? What did you learn?

Listening

1.) Read "The Summer Day" by Mary Oliver. The poem says, "I don't know, exactly, what a prayer is. / I do know how to pay attention . . . ." What do these words mean? What might be the relationship between praying and paying attention?

2.) Can objects in the real world be speaking to us? Does "meaning" come from inside us or from outside? Are there various ways of speaking? Of listening?

3.) What can be the value of wonder? Of ambiguity? Of mystery? (See: "When I Heard the Learn'd Astronomer" by Walt Whitman.)

4.) In the play *Someday I'd Write This Down*, how is the narrator's story also your story?

Prompt: Imagine that you are an omniscient being looking down on the earth and watching people come and go. Write about what you might see and how you might struggle to understand what it means to be human.

Suggestions for Teachers:

— Have students read the poem aloud. Read it slowly, and read it more than once.

— Encourage discussion. Ask open-ended questions.
> "How does the title help us understand the poem?"
> "Does the poem tell a story?"
> "What do you picture in your mind when you hear this poem?"
> "How does the poem want you to respond?"

— Allow students some quiet time to think and reflect.
> Ask: "Have you experienced anything like the poem is talking about?"

— Read the prompt aloud.

— Try a five minute "free-write" in which students write as quickly as possible.
> Ask: "What words, images, or stories does the prompt make you think about?"
> These will serve as notes to begin shaping a poem.

— Guide students to understand that there is no single "right" way to write a poem.
> Every poem is an experiment. But . . . this doesn't mean that every poem is a
> success. Readers can gauge whether the poem is enjoyable, meaningful. If
> readers are confused by the poem, use this feedback to encourage the poet to
> revise and clarify.

— Try a poetry "coffee house" in which students present their poems to an
> audience of their classmates.

Encourage Students to Rewrite, Rework, Revise:

— Does the poem need more details and specifics? Details and specifics help the reader
> to "see" in their mind's eye what the poem is describing. An image is a picture
> in the imagination. We say, "A picture is worth a thousand words." In this way,
> images can help a poem say important or powerful things with only a few words.

— Help students understand the difference between abstract language and concrete
> language. Images are built on concrete language — details and specifics.
> "No ideas but in things," said the poet William Carlos Williams. Poems
> use concrete details to coax readers into abstract realizations.

— The poet Coleridge defined poetry as "the best words in the best order." Encourage
> students to look closely at the language of the poem. Are there unnecessary
> words? Are the words of the poem fresh and interesting? Encourage students to
> identify and eliminate clichés. Challenge students to find new ways of saying
> things. Use a thesaurus to find the best word, not the biggest word.

— Rhyming is often the only type of poem students know. Allow them to rhyme if
> they must, but encourage students to try "free verse" poetry, poetry without
> rhyme. In revising a rhyming poem, ask students to identify where the rhyming
> seems awkward or forced. Where does the rhyming twist or distort the poem's
> meaning?

— Encourage students to see their poems as experiments. Scientists view a failed experiment not as failure but as the next step toward discovery. No poem is perfect; with effort, all poems can be improved. Encourage a "growth mindset" (See: *Mindset* by Carol Dwek).

— Encourage students to give their poem a title. A good title can tune the reader into the appropriate "channel" to best understand or experience what the poem has to say.

— Ambiguity in a poem can allow the reader to appreciate the poem in many ways. But . . . too much ambiguity will harm the poem's communication. Resist the all-too-common misconception that a poem "means whatever you want it to mean." What words, phrases, lines, stanzas seem vague or confusing?

— Ask the poet to consider the reader. "How do you want the reader to react to this poem?" "Does this poem accomplish what it is intending to accomplish?"

— Laurence Perrine, in his famous text *Sound and Sense*, defined poetry as the "recreation of experience." This means that the poem should be an experience for the reader; the reader should be participating in the poem rather than just listening. "Show, don't tell," is a popular aphorism among writing teachers. "Showing" is accomplished by giving readers specifics and details and letting readers use those cues to make connections on their own. Novice writers want to simply "tell" the reader about a thought or a feeling.

— Spelling and grammar are important considerations. Grammatical errors and misspelling can distract or confuse the reader. Encourage students to practice saying thank you when someone points out an error.

— Encourage students to read poems. Make poetry a daily practice in your classroom. The website poetryfoundation.org is rich with resources for teachers and readers of poetry. Also, YouTube has a wide selection of poets reading and performing. These can be valuable models for students to emulate.

Lowell Jaeger (Montana Poet Laureate 2017-2019) is a graduate of the Iowa Writers' Workshop, winner of the Grolier Poetry Peace Prize, and recipient of fellowships from the National Endowment for the Arts and the Montana Arts Council. He has taught creative writing at Flathead Valley Community College (Kalispell, Montana) for the past 35 years, and he has also been self-employed for many years as a silversmith/goldsmith. In 2010, Jaeger was awarded the Montana Governor's Humanities Award for his work in promoting civil civic discourse.

Also by Lowell Jaeger:

Earth-blood & Star-shine (Shabda Press, 2018)
Or Maybe I Drift Off Alone (Shabda Press, 2016)
Driving the Back Road Home (Shabda Press, 2015)
How Quickly What's Passing Goes Past (Grayson Books, 2013)
WE (Main Street Rag Publishing, 2010)
Suddenly Out of a Long Sleep (Arctos Press, 2009)
Hope Against Hope (Utah State University Press, 1990)
War On War (Utah State University Press, 1988)

Edited by Lowell Jaeger and Hannah Bissell Kauffman:

Poems Across the Big Sky II (Many Voices Press, 2017)
New Poets of the American West (Many Voices Press, 2010)
Poems Across the Big Sky (Many Voices Press, 2007)